Stephanie

Madagascar:
The Window of My Soul

*May God's truth be
the window of your soul
as you celebrate God and
scatter joy!*

Madagascar:
The Window of My Soul

Patricia McGregor

Xulon Press

Xulon Press
2301 Lucien Way #415
Maitland, FL 32751
407.339.4217
www.xulonpress.com

Unless otherwise indicated, Scripture quotations taken from the Holy Bible, New International Version (NIV). Copyright © 1973, 1978, 1984, 2011 by Biblica, Inc.™. Used by permission. All rights reserved.

Paperback ISBN-13: 978-1-66285-551-1
Ebook ISBN-13: 978-1-66285-552-8

Dedication

To the Malagasy people who have embraced me
with love, joy and and an open spirit,
welcoming us as their own.

Table of Contents

Dedication v

Foreword ix

Introduction xi

Chapter One: COURAGE 1

Chapter Two: CALLING 21

Chapter Three: CHARACTER 43

Chapter Four: CHEMISTRY 75

Chapter Five: COMPETENCY 95

Chapter Six: COMMUNITY 119

Epilogue: Madagascar: The Window of My Soul 139

Timeline 143

Study Guide 149

Acknowledgements 161

Appendix A 163

Appendix B 175

Appendix C 183

Bibliography 187

Endnotes 191

Foreword

S ome time back, when I was on study tour in Israel, with a group of Bible translation consultants, a lady from a Bruderhof Community in the United States joined our dinner table and asked where I came from. When I said I lived in Madagascar, her eyes lit up. "Oh, that's interesting!" I expected the next question to be either about what I do there, or about the amazing flora and fauna in Madagascar. But instead, fixing her eyes on mine, she asked, "And how has living in Madagascar changed you?" Well, no one's asked me that before! And I still haven't finished answering.

Patsy and I have talked a lot on our Friday afternoon COVID-19 – distanced walks among the cacti of the spiny desert here in Toliara. We have pondered how God has used this beautifully challenging country, and her beautifully challenging people, to teach us more about Himself, and to change us to become more like Him.

We have learned so much from our Malagasy friends: about faith in the face of relentless poverty and disasters like cyclones, cholera, famine and COVID-19; about respecting people, and valuing relationships more than getting-things-done; about humility and putting others first. The list could go on.....

Patsy and Todd have faced enormous challenges in every possible domain, and God has not only changed them, but He's used them as His agents to bring about change for the increase of His kingdom. I've learned much – and been changed by – listening to Patsy's fresh joy-filled insights about God and the way He works. She's delightful to spend time with, as you'll discover for yourself, as we walk these dusty cactus-lined roads together.

Bev Erasmus
Wycliffe Bible Translator
Toliara, Madagascar
November, 2020

Introduction

T he rooster crowed, and I rose at 4:30 a.m. It was the day of my husband's consecration as Assistant Bishop of Antananarivo to lead the creation of the future Diocese of Toliara. I grabbed my Bible and tiptoed out of our bedroom to spend time with God.

Reading Jesus' parable about the widow who had only two, very small copper coins,[1] I reflected on the similarity to my own story. My husband was being consecrated as a bishop and we would be moving to Toliara, Madagascar. He had a multitude of dreams, goals, passion and excitement. Not me, however. I felt I did not have much to offer and could relate to the desperate widow and her two small coins.

Based on my experiences and eleven years of previously living in Madagascar, I recognized I would be once again going into a battleground. Hardships of the spiny desert and profound poverty were just a few of the challenges of living in this arid cactus-filled environment. Instead of the lush vibrant tropical landscapes that nurtured me in Antananarivo and Kenya, I would encounter barren sunbaked land with sparse vegetation. Instead of being in a place I blossomed and thrived, I would regularly encounter abject poverty, drought, famine and spiritual warfare. This created not only physical but spiritual barrenness. Knowing it required emotional grit, I feared it would suck my energy. My task was daunting.

On top of this, I had just been ordained and would be going back to a spiritual environment that did not welcome women as priests. And while I knew I had gifts and talents, I wondered whether they would be appreciated. I felt like the widow, who had no reserve giving all she had. Symbolically, placing two small coins in my palms, I lifted my hands to God. *Lord, I do not have much, but what I do have, I give to you. Here is my heart, my desire to serve You and my aspiration to see Your people come to know You.*

While I thought I only had two small coins, God saw opportunities and potential in me that I did not know I had. Passion grew in different areas. Unknown gifts began to bloom and I lived into a larger self that God knew was there all along. My nurturing heart became a pastoral fire, desiring for people to grow in their walk with the Lord. Prayer-walking the city and praying-in-color[2] allowed for an active and creative prayer life which became foundations of the life we shared with our neighbors. People began to join us as we prayed-in-color. The Shaman's daughter expressed interest in Christianity and began prayer-walking the city with us, bringing other neighbors alongside.

Praying-in-color allowed non-threatening prayers to be lifted for the community. Markers, index cards and a boom box playing Christian music attracted passersby carrying straw mats on the top of their heads to escape the noonday heat and nap under the sacred tree. Invited to join us, they found interest in the creative prayer language or was it first because they often held markers in their hands for the first time?

As we lived the Great Commandment, we emphasized a relational style of evangelism through the Great Commission of loving God and loving our neighbors as ourselves. Love, only love, is the core of Jesus' incarnational ministry and it became the core of ours.

Memoirs from our first eleven years in Madagascar can be read in my first book, *A Guest In God's World.* My book *Tamana,* includes the first three and one-half years of our relational ministry in Toliara. Our neighbor was a local animistic priest of the African Traditional Religion, known as a *shaman.* Remamy, *the shaman,* became our friend and protector during a political coup.

We had an up-close and personal friendship with him and specifically one of his several children, Nolavy, a nineteen-year-old girl at the time. Living as neighbors, Todd and I gained the *shaman's* trust. Remamy ultimately surrendered all spiritual authority of his daughter to Todd and me. After many years of discipleship and education, Nolavy became the first woman ordained as an Anglican priest in the Diocese of Toliara and after much deliberation, Remamy also received Christ as his Lord and Savior.

And now, as I come to the end of our story, my fingers freeze. Not physically, because it is summer in Madagascar and 94 degrees outside. Since there is no central air conditioning, the house isn't much cooler. Emotionally, the sinews and tendons fail to dance on the keyboard as they have with other writings. More like fingers of an old woman pained with arthritis, joints feel inflamed. I want to skip this transition...this uncertain and yet daunting chapter of life.

With only six weeks remaining, Todd and I are saying goodbye to a country and its people with whom we have lived almost three decades. Embracing us as their own, the Malagasy people have caused us to become *tamana*, at home, in a place in which I thought I never could settle or be comfortable, much less be changed by living in Madagascar.

Frustratingly difficult years of challenge have been softened with love, purpose and meaning. Genuinely indebted for assistance given to themselves, their families, their churches and their country, gracious Malagasy have in return, graced us with their hearts. The kindness, generosity, hospitality, joy and love of the Malagasy people have soaked deep into my veins. I have been blessed.

When we purchased the property and first developed the Master Plan for the Cathedral Complex for the Diocese of Toliara, there was hardly a bush growing on the hard, salt laden ground. Before trees, bees, and bougainvillea, before the labyrinth, a wall, the Women's Center, Gathering Place, Bible School, Dormitory or Cathedral, there was the first building, the Educational Center. Soon after the building was completed, a friend of mine came on a short-term mission trip. Since she was an interior designer, I took advantage of her expertise.

"If this were your office, Cheryl, how would you place the furniture?"

"It all starts with the desk, Patsy, since that is where you will sit many hours of the day. What do you want to look at? What do you want your perspective to be?"

"I want to look at people as they come into the door. I want to look at them, and when there is no one in my office, I want to look at Toliara's Table Mountain."

Life is all about perspective. As you go through life, what do you want to look at? What do you want your perspective to be? "The real voyage of discovery consists not in seeking new landscapes, but in having new eyes."[3]

For me, Madagascar has been my landscape, my frame of reference. It has been the way through which I have perceived the world. Living in Madagascar has given me deep set eyes. This beautifully challenging and unique country has become the *window of my soul.*

Change is difficult. When flying from point A to point B, we sometimes want to skip the hard part of traveling – the process - and get to the destination. Not only do we have the necessity of packing and lugging heavy suitcases, but also the clumsiness of going through metal detectors and security checks. And then… the long hours of waiting until we arrive at our destination. Even more troubling are the goodbyes, the uncertainties, and uncomfortable emotions along the way. Specifically at this period of time, the COVID-19 pandemic has stretched our elasticity. Tired and weary, we are now forced to say goodbye to friends and co-workers without proper ceremony – No visit, no handshake, no hug.

Martin Luther King, Jr. said, "If you can't fly, then run. If you can't run, then walk. If you can't walk, crawl, but whatever you do, you have to keep moving forward."[4] How can we move forward when our hearts have been left behind?

Chapter One

COURAGE

Have I not commanded you?
Be strong and courageous.
Do not be terrified; do not be discouraged,
for the Lord your God will be with you wherever you go.
Joshua 1:9

"I'm Praying for You!"

I t was our first goodbye. Due to government restraints from the COVID-19 pandemic, we were not able to travel for our annual pastoral visit including confirmations, baptisms, and marriages. Considering a parish within the Diocese of Toliara may be a three-day drive away, the Malagasy parishioners excitedly anticipate these visits.

Knowing it would be our last time to visit these parishes after forming the Diocese of Toliara out of the Diocese of Antananarivo and living in the south of the Red Island for fourteen years, we needed a strategy. Some of the clergy brainstormed together with my bishop-husband on how to still meet together under the COVID restrictions of no local travel, no more than 50 people gathering in one building remaining one meter apart. They came up with the idea to Zoom on the scheduled day of the Bishop's visit. This type of technology was a rarity in most parts of Madagascar.

Up to this time, people in the Diocese were still holding their regular services, Todd and I 'Zoomed' in for the service. The parish priest, Rev. Nolavy and her husband Rev. Victor, concelebrated communion. Todd gave the sermon, absolution, final blessing and we both gave words of gratitude and goodbye. My last words to the church in Sakaraha were, *Mivavaka ho anao aho. I'm praying for you.*

And then, as God would have it, someone on the keyboard spontaneously began to play the tune and the parishioners broke out in chorus, singing the words to our first song written for the *Miaraka: A Time to Dance* musical. [5] A tear slid down my cheek and my mind flashed back to our first airplane journey to Madagascar, twenty-nine years earlier.

Jomo Kenyatta International Airport, Nairobi, August 1991

Staring at the barrel of the gun, I was courageous and determined. Metal detectors, military police and machine guns would not deter us from getting to Madagascar. Due to mix-ups and confusion, airport personnel had told us the wrong gate number for the flight to Madagascar. With only minutes to spare, I ran through the airport with our elder daughter in a stroller. Finally getting to Gate 1, there was not a person in sight. I crashed the gate, threw open the exit door and ran down the ramp, onto the tarmac. In front of the Air Madagascar plane, I stood firm and commanded. "STOP THAT PLANE!"

Surprised, peering down from the cockpit, the pilot removed his headphones and tried to communicate to me through body language. Certainly, I did not appear to be a terrorist. Accompanied by military police pointing machine guns at my chest, questioning airport personnel, approached me. What was this 31 year old redheaded white woman pushing a baby in a stroller doing on the runway? Strong-minded and unwavering, I was determined to go to Madagascar. You can read more about this incredible story of God's hand on our first journey in my first memories, *A Guest in God's World.*

I didn't necessarily realize it when I stopped the plane with our twenty-seven month old daughter in her stroller, but the Spirit of the Lord was upon us. The Lord had anointed us to preach good news to the poor, to bind up the brokenhearted, to proclaim freedom for the captives and release prisoners from darkness.[6]

That notorious plane ride put us into the unknown arena of Madagascar; the lion's den of hard work and spiritual warfare. With the insecure feeling of being constantly out of place, we adapted to a foreign culture and a new language. Naive and unknowing, we lived in a new land where we couldn't predict or control the outcome.

Courage underpins brave leadership. And it's a command, just like the other 613 directives in the Old Testament. "Have I not commanded you? Be strong and courageous. Do not be afraid; do not be discouraged, for the Lord your God will be with you wherever you go."[7]

The plane ride memory faded and I once again was in the present moment, on a "zoom" church service speaking Malagasy. Oh my, how much has evolved over these past twenty-nine years. Friendships formed, cathedrals built, health clinics and schools created offering hope, people's lives transformed, all because of God's grace and courageous call to be with us wherever we go...and God's ever-present promise to be praying for us!

Spiritual Tug-of-War

God has designs on our lives long before we begin seeking him. His design for us is glorious living. His purpose embraces and enfolds us, helping us to understand ourselves, giving meaning to our lives. And yet, life is a battle-waging challenge filled with hardship and suffering. Paul reminds us of this spiritual tug-of-war, telling us to be completely confident in the gospel.[8] God does the saving. We do the believing. God does the leading. We do the following. Response is our choice.

Early one morning I had a dream that a bazooka was aimed smack-dab at my husband. It's not the first time I have had such a strong dream about battles. Being a missionary has put us in the trenches. Are we tenacious enough to face hefty spiritual warfare, internal struggles, and be leaders in our communities in the midst of discomfort? Courage and fear are not mutually exclusive.[9] Feeling fear is not the barrier, but rather, how do we respond to our fear?

I have met missionaries and cross-cultural workers who have had a desire to go to a certain country and lead a specific people group. Desperately I have urged some to come partner with us in Madagascar. It is not uncommon to receive an answer like this. "I don't have a heart for those people." Bristling at their comment, I wonder, "How do you know until you go?" How do we develop caring and connection with people we have never met?

Humanity of church leadership and global ministry is messy. There are fears, feelings, and social skills that get in the way. Most importantly, we need courage and vulnerability to go into the arena and give it our best shot. Sometimes, all we need to do is show up.

Our adventures and experiences of life during times of uncertainty, risk and emotional exposure[10] take courage. Leadership is taking responsibility for finding potential in others – for identifying the gifts, talents and treasures in people and processes, and supporting the people who have the courage to develop their own potential. Perhaps we weren't fully aware at the time, but it took courage and trust to cross an ocean, bravely taking two small children to live in another country.

And it has taken courage and perseverance to live three decades as cross-cultural workers in Madagascar, Kenya and Mauritius.

"It's not what you do, it's why you do it that makes a difference."[11] It is only with others that we have been able to fulfill our mission in community and be People Reaching People. The Malagasy culture is an amazing community. Our many friendships have blossomed throughout the years, blessing us in ways that we would have never imagined.

Ready?

On her first day of kindergarten, our younger daughter, Charese, was ready. Although she was still sleeping when I walked into her room that early morning in Boca Raton, Florida, (we were on a nine-month furlough) she had gotten up in the middle of the night, put on her school uniform and crawled back into bed, falling asleep. Like a fireman ready for the alarm, shoes were by her backpack. She was ready.

I too, am usually ready. According to the Clifton Strengths Finder Indicator, I am an Activator; a strategic organizer who plans for the future, ready to activate upon the word, "Go."[12]

But once in Madagascar, it took a while for me to process my "Activating" strength. When Todd and I were pondering global ministry, we hesitated. "Go? Where? Why? When? How Come?" And as we leave Madagascar and return to the USA three decades later, we again ask the same questions: "Go? Where? Why? When? How Come?"

The truth is, life is a constant flow of situations, ever changing. Transition is also an inward journey. All international and most local travel was ceased due to the Coronavirus in 2020, providing more time for introspection and preparation. I found time to process thirty years in the arena. Wow! When I stopped the plane on the runway that life-changing August day in 1991, I never thought we would be on a life- journey of long plane rides across oceans and continents. And I never thought I would be leaving three decades later.

What have we learned?
What have we taught?
Why has it worked?
How has it been meaningful?
How have we been blessed?
Why is it hard to leave?

"Some people run away from grief, go on world cruises or move to another town. But they do not escape. The memories, unbidden, spring into their minds, scattered perhaps over the years. There is something to be said for facing them all deliberately and straight away."[13]

Scary and yet life-giving, our new challenge was not another cathedral to build or another program to implement, rather to patiently bear sorrow, and gather and give blessings as good-byes were said. Grief is a form of love.

Grieving loss openly, honestly and together can strengthen and broaden perspective. The Malagasy people taught us what it means to live in a world of joy mixed with pain and disappointment while abiding in communities of blessing. We are not exempt from life's frailties but have the choice to embrace our experiences and use them to grow stronger, carrying them together, blessed by walking hand in hand with friends and loved ones.

Are your shoes by the door? Are you ready to join hands and walk together, brave enough to bless and be blessed? Come! Let's go!

Our Brave Worship Walk

The unmarked path took us across mounds of mud. Clods of muck and zebu droppings from the cattle ahead clung to our shoes as we cautiously retained balance, delicately trying not to slip and fall. Five-year-old Benjamin, walking through mud, sand and cactus in southwest Madagascar, spoke a truth. "I'm brave."

Wouldn't it be enriching if all of us were this confident? After all, aren't we all brave as we worship-walk the path of life? With uniqueness, we all have our own heroic stories of valor. Stepping out into the unmarked path of life requires strength, perseverance and determination.

God calls us to come – just as we are – wounded and tired, courageously exposing our vulnerability and wounds to God's healing light. The road of life is long, weather beaten. It is essential to spend ample time saturating in the presence of God fully opened to his living presence. Being placed outdoors in sunlight and fresh air for hours at a time has successfully treated many people who are seriously ill. Similarly, we need substantial time soaking in God's grace and presence to heal deep wounds.

Realizing our blessings harvests the fruit of our labor. Fleeing to God gives us great confidence as we hold onto hope that lies before us. Hope is a strong and trustworthy anchor for our souls, leading us to God's inner sanctuary.[14]

Life takes courage. It took bravery and grit to sit next to my father as his frail body became weaker and more fragile. Helpless and powerless, I watched God prepare my father's soul for that sanctuary of eternal life. A mixture of blessing and anguish, it was joyous and heart wrenching at the same time.

God's wisdom and ways are utterly beyond our comprehension, only giving us glimpses of glory. This inspires us to worship-walk. Bowing before the infinite intelligence and limitless power of God, we open our souls in worship, dancing in God's sunlight, realizing we are brave, assured in God's unfailing love. God speaks. We listen. *I know the plans I have for you, plans to prosper you and not to harm you, plans to give you hope and a future.*[15]

For You, O Lord, bless the righteous; with favor you surround him as with a shield.[16] Let's harvest these blessings. Come! Let's discover what God has done in us, and through us and around us. Even if we're deep in cow dung, we are brave!

And now, back in the USA, I'm reminded to worship-walk. It's not cow dung and spiny cactus that cling to my shoes, but other sticky substances. Pressures, deadlines, pastoral emergencies cause a hurried gate to my stride. As I go, I'm reminded to worship as I walk, for if ever I am too busy to worship, I am too busy.

Brave to go.

Brave to return.

Brave to give.

Brave to receive.

Brave to bless.

Brave to be blessed.

In all situations, brave to worship-walk the path of life.

Picking the Poppies

A few years ago a friend had a vision while praying for me; there I was, in a green, grassy meadow, with Jesus by my side. Content and joyous, I was picking poppies, making a bouquet and giving it to Jesus, my friend and my companion.

Why poppies? I googled 'poppies.' A common sight in the landscapes of the First World War, red poppies are the enduring symbol of remembrance and hope; the vivid red of the poppies symbolizes the military comrades' blood soaking into the battleground. I could relate. I felt my missionary blood was soaking into the battleground of Madagascar.

War torn and battered, it's not uncommon for global workers to come back from the field with anxiety and tension from constant stress. For myself, I have termed it PMSS, Post Missionary Stress Syndrome or more personally, Patsy's Missionary Stress Syndrome. Don't get me wrong; there are tremendous blessings harvesting God's work in the mission field. But many times we come back from the battlefield broken, bruised, scarred and limping.

Several years ago, a friend gave me a little music box. The song played, "What a Wonderful World." Turning the small handle, she sang the words.

> I see trees of green, red roses too.
> I see them bloom, for me and you.
> And I think to myself,
> What a wonderful world.[17]

With fatigue, exhaustion and difficult situations penetrating my soul, I had lost the feeling that it was a wonderful world. I had seen too much hardship, poverty, famine, sickness, death and dying. I needed God to refresh my perspective and remind me, it *is* a wonderful world. I needed a divine reversal.

Whatever our circumstances of life, divine reversals are part of God's plan. God promises to work out all things for good for those who love God and for those who are called according to his purpose.[18] Hardships gain meaning, challenges strengthen us, problems bring patient endurance and we become brave. God's plans will not be thwarted.

Caring for my father at my parents' home during my dad's last month of earthly life, I found myself praying in all forms, mostly without intelligible words, as the grief was too much to bear. Hand sewn white angel wing prayer flags, sent by a friend in Minnesota, fluttered in mom and dad's room, a reminder of God's constant presence and the angels' continual guard and protection, every moment, every day.

Waving, the flags were a constant prayer; audible words were way too difficult for me to express after dad took a fall. Mom and I nervously made a great team, lifting dad off the bathroom floor at 4:00 am. Dad had escaped his bed without our knowing. He quietly and valiantly made his way to the bathroom and then lost his balance. This was another indication of his frailty, and with this reality, I found it hard to concentrate. Reading a book or even glancing at the Book of Common Prayer seemed out of the question. So, I prayed while doing a jigsaw, the puzzle process calming me as my wandering mind pleaded, and my hands interlocked pieces of the giraffe...or was it a piece of the elephant...or maybe it was a baboon after all?

During COVID-19 as we were in transition from our missionary life in Madagascar, Todd and I had several large 1000-piece puzzles on the dining room table in the center of our living space. We didn't assemble them on a side table, but rather smack dab in the middle of our everyday life, a metaphor of the puzzling time we and the world were going through. After sorting the pieces and interlocking the border, some puzzles were as large as the table. With no space to place the spare pieces, kitchen trays were stacked on bar stools, puzzle pieces everywhere.

The whole process seemed to be in disarray. Much like some seasons of life, how could we make sense of it all?

Taking us to the core of our beings, challenging situations can help us identify, purpose, substance, faith. God wants us to be brave. Since God works out everything for good, divine reversal is part of God's Will. Resilient and courageous, God strengthens our hearts with hope and red poppies begin adorning the fields, popping up everywhere.

Divine Reversal

I have found when life gets overwhelming, I try and see things from God's point of view. A few days before my father's imminent passing, I wrote in my journal. Written with God's perspective in mind, it helped me to see the divine reversal.

Thank you, for coming to Me with a courageous heart. I know these upcoming few days could be filled with anxiety, from the world's view, but worry not! I have overcome the world. Major transitions will occur within the next few days. Your father will pass and come to the house I have prepared for him. It won't be easy, but it will be good. It will make you feel sad and ecstatic at the same time. You will feel a huge void that only I can fill. It will be a day like never before. Peace, I have for you, not as the world gives, but as I give. I have overcome the world. I have prepared you for this day. Be strong and courageous.

I felt the Lord continuing to speak...

Being strong and courageous doesn't mean your heart is without emotion. No, not at all. Rather, it means that your heart is secure, trusting, unwavering. Continue in a strong and steady way; constantly, steadfastly. This is My Will for you. Doubt is normal in the world's view but it is contrary to trust. A lack of confidence can plague even the strongest Christians. More personally, it can

13

plague you, killing the Spirit within you. Please, continue on your journey. Move ahead.

Your life is in My Hands. Thank you, precious, princess warrior, for praying My Will to be done. This prayer shows your heart's desire – to do My Will and follow Me, wherever I lead you. I am so proud of you.

The tendency is to be anxious. This is normal. But fear not. I am with you. I have planned this. Run...into My Arms...I am here for you, my precious, redheaded girl.

Taking a deep breath, oxygen infused my soul. Exhaling, I let out a loud sigh. Hearing a blessing from God anchored me. We can strengthen our muscles and strengthen our brains, but only God strengthens the heart. Be of good courage, and He shall strengthen your heart, all you who hope in the Lord.[19]

It takes courage to allow God to go into the hidden corners of our minds. But God is gentle, tending his flock like a shepherd. He carries the lambs in his arms and carries them close to his heart; gently leading those that have young.[20]

A few days later, on Monday, December 2nd 2019 at 12:58 pm, Dad passed away. It was beautiful and heart wrenching at the same time. My heart flip-flopped, held a void, a vacuum, only to be filled with God. Finally regaining strength three days later, I wrote my first journal entry after Dad's passing.

I've been brave, courageous. I've been a nurse, daughter, sister, priest. It's been an excruciating few days. Now, I'm exhausted. My body cramps, my mind is restless, my soul and spirit numb. And I feel the peace of God brushing my forehead saying "That's okay."

Courage to Love

Sharing our faith is a challenge. Theologically the term is the 'Great Commission.' We are told to go into all the world and share the gospel.

It takes courage to love people and share our faith. Implementing the Great Commandment (loving our neighbor as ourselves,) can be even harder than proclaiming the Great Commission (sharing our faith.) Learning from others and loving them is a process. This takes courage, no matter where we are in the world.

It takes courage to love. Sharing our faith and inviting others into our life takes courage. Living shoulder-to-shoulder takes vulnerability, transparency, fullness of heart and mind. There is simply no substitute for being with people. Sharing our faith with others and living a transparent lifestyle is a strong cord, not easily broken. This is the Great Commandment. "Loving the Lord with all our hearts, soul and minds and loving our neighbors as ourselves.[21] Rubbing shoulders with our neighbors, we learn to love.

Living among the Malagasy people in Ankilifaly as well as living eleven years in the capital of Madagascar, Antananarivo, we were keenly aware of a society that strongly trusts in a unique form of ancestor worship.

My faith was challenged and strengthened by this unique form of ancestor worship. I really needed to be firmly established in my Christian beliefs, believing Jesus is our greatest ancestor. Believing Jesus is our mediator been God and human beings, I could understand the Malagasy culture desiring someone to mediate for them before God. My answer is jesus and they were very receptive to the idea. Our Christianity enhanced their innate belief system, honoring God and one another. God was always showing up. Daily God-moments were experienced as people worshiped the Lord freely.

Society thrives because of love. Jesus loved people and loved spending time with them. From the gospels, it is obvious that Jesus enjoyed being with seekers far more than being with religious leaders. We must love others the way Jesus did. Love draws people like a magnet. A lack of love drives them away. Loving others the way Jesus would takes courage.

Courage to Care

Desperate, Malala rose before the sun, spending an hour walking to the water hole before sand baked beneath her toes. Perspiration beaded her brow, even at the early morning hour. Finally arriving at her destination, she found only a trickle of water, the source running dry. Lack of rain for two years had taken a toll on the land, not to mention the destruction by the locusts that ate the small crop that had somehow managed to sprout above the barren earth. Devastated, she returned to her one-room thatched hut with a partially filled bucket of water from which her family would bathe, drink and cook.

In southwestern regions of Madagascar, villages go for long periods of time, several months, sometimes years, without even light precipitation. When rain finally does come, people of all ages flock to a dip in the land. Taking a torn rag, men, women and children soak up rain water, pouring it into their mouths and onto their faces. Hastily placing buckets on the ground, they pray, hopeful to gather a bit of extra water needed for upcoming days. When rainwater runs dry, the vicious cycle begins again.

This is a culture quite different from the Treasure Coast of Southeast Florida, where I am a canonical resident and Episcopal priest.

Culture is the world into which a person is born and the world which in turn, is born into that person. Culture can be defined as one's perspective of the world. That perspective shapes a person and their worldview. It alters what is said and heard, and how words are communicated. It is an ethos, an outlook, a point of view.

For me, culture includes my birthplace, America, and the world that has been born into me, Madagascar. It includes access to water and electricity and economics, money, wealth, poverty, politics, demographics and technology. It can be primitive. During my 30 years of missionary life, mostly in Madagascar, some Malagasy have experienced increased access to daily life-giving resources. However, Madagascar continues to be one of the poorest countries in the world. Nation-wide, approximately 58% of all Malagasy have access to clean water, 14% of all households have electricity, and 12% have an indoor flush toilet.[22] For me, culture also includes another extreme. Many of those living in an economically advantaged country can have almost anything they want, albeit for a price, including invitro-fertilization and a gender change.

As a missionary, I've dealt with extremes of culture. Traveling from country to country, my family and I have experienced the ambiguous world of "culture shock." In Madagascar, our community resided in one of the poorest areas in one of the poorest countries in the world. Ninety percent of our friends and neighbors lived off an income of less than one dollar a day. Some made their living off the plastic water bottles our short-term mission teams drank and discarded. Others sold a few rusty nails, nuts or bolts to help purchase rice for their family of nine. Statistics show that only 30% of the children in Madagascar complete primary school and the literacy rate is approximately 65%. In the south, a heavily rural area, there is even less access to education.

Culture includes traditions, background, customs and ethnicity. It determines how people live and interact with others, how they define themselves and how they communicate with others. Culture causes a person to look around and be watchful, observing situations at hand.

Like unseen molecules in the air, culture exists and forms our being. Like melting snow, culture cannot be grasped nor held in the palm of our hands. It is one's perspective, a way of life, a perception largely self-created. It is a learned pattern of attitudes, values, customs, and beliefs.

It takes courage to care for others in any culture. Love wants us to be sensitive to the needs of those around, and show compassion to those next door. "Jesus taught us the evidence of love. It's found in seeing a need in others, then doing all we can to satisfy it."[23] "For I was hungry, and you gave Me something to eat; I was thirsty, and you gave Me something to drink; I was a stranger, and you invited Me in; naked, and you clothed Me; I was sick, and you visited Me; I was in prison, and you came to Me"[24]

Love beyond borders. Love moves us beyond ourselves and turns our attention to another's need. Anywhere. Everywhere. Love makes sacrifices.

Reflections

Grant us patience, O Lord, to follow the
road you have taken.
Let our confidence not rest in our own understanding
but in your guiding hand;
let our desires not be for our own comfort, but for
the joy of your kingdom;
for your cross is our hope and our joy now and unto
the day of eternity. *Amen.*

Saint Augustine's Prayer Book,
published by Forward Movement in 2013.

Christians are to be good news before they share the good news. The words of the gospel are to be lived out and verbalized. Many in current society will most likely not step inside a church door. They look at Christians to see Jesus. Do you look like Jesus to others? How does living a transparent and authentic lifestyle help you to be a witness to your neighbors?

Two great forces in lifestyle evangelism are a healthy church and healthy family relationships. The Christian family in a community is an ultimate evangelistic tool. A healthy home circle is an open book, allowing the beauty of the gospel to shine light into the surrounding community. When love is seen, the message is heard. What are some practical ways that God's message is seen through you?

Chapter Two

CALLING

Let each one examine their own work,
and then they will have rejoicing.
Galatians 6:4

Hiding?

C alling, like courage, starts with little steps. Calming an upset teenager, fixing food for a sick neighbor or molding Play Doh with a two-year old. Calling begins with experiencing

God in the everyday. Bargaining for bananas were my first steps of walking into my calling.

"*Hoootrinona*?" (How much?) I stuttered.

Immediately she grinned, ear to ear. "*Ahh! Mahay miteny Malagasy!*" (*Oh, you speak Malagasy!*) Returning her smile, I left the bananas and continued my way, wondering what more she said. Upon returning home I consulted the dictionary and chuckled. Sometimes our daily calling is as unique as learning a new sentence.

For entertainment in Toliara, my husband and I watch DVDs of television series carried over in our suitcases. *Castle* was a favorite, especially since we gleaned relational methods of a woman cop, Becket, and a male writer, Castle, working together in spite of very different personalities. Finding plenty of time during the COVID season, we watched all eight seasons and then started another show, *Person of Interest.*

Season 1 Episode 1 set the tone. John Reese, a former US Navy SEAL returned from the field, disappointed, disillusioned and experiencing PTSD. In despair, he became a reclusive, homeless drunkard, living on the streets for eight months. Then wealthy, intelligent, techie Harold Finch, maker of "the machine" needed help. To save the person of interest, he pursued Reese to work with him. Knowing he had lost hope, Reese wondered if he could still be of use. Finch assured him, he didn't need pills, or therapy, all he needed was purpose.

Like Reese, perhaps it would be easiest to receive a call from Harold Finch, reminding us who we are and no matter our circumstances, we are made for a purpose. Each one of us has a call to use our talents to the glory of God in service to one another. God is the One who is leading us on the road of life, calling us to reach out and be of assistance to our communities.

One definition of leader is "anyone who takes responsibility for finding the potential in people and processes, and who has the courage to develop that potential."[25] Just as Reese was sought out and found by Harold Finch, the nature of calling is that we are also sought out and found by God. The job is always too big for our own selves and we depend on teamwork.

The absurdity of calling is that we don't know what we're getting ourselves into. When we first came to Madagascar with our two small children, we did not have the slightest inkling we would stay thirty years and build a new diocese from the ground up. Anticipating three, maybe six years at most, we responded to a call with little steps. Only God takes us from fearful hiding to victory. Gideon's response was low in trust, to say the least. Let's look at a holy dialogue between God and Gideon.[26]

God: *"The Lord is with you brave and mighty man."*

Gideon: *"The Lord has abandoned us and left us to the mercy of the Midianites."*

God: *Go with all your strength. I am sending you.*

Gideon: *How can I?*

God: *You can do it because I will help you.*

Gideon: *If you are pleased with me, give me some proof.*

Scripture calls us living epistles. No matter what culture we live in, our lives are to be testimonies to God's goodness and grace. Theologically speaking, it's called Orthopraxy.[27] Simplicity calls it right living. With Scripture as our plumb line to measure truth, we can live into our calling, because God has called us.[28]

Perhaps like Reese and Gideon, some of us are hiding. Unsure and doubting, we question our purpose. But calling, like courage, requires our first small step. Starting now, in the present situation, we discover the path God has for us. Finally, when found, like Gideon, we fall to our knees and worship.[29]

Why Not?

Todd's call was apparent to me even before he knew my name. Attending New Covenant Church in Pompano Beach, Florida, Todd was leader for youth and singles. In a large congregation of over a thousand, we didn't cross paths often, but I could see his gifting. I knew he was called. In fact, it scared me. Prophetically believing God may bring us together, I didn't want to be involved in full-time ministry. I wanted to marry a Christian businessman who would earn a good salary and give me a fairy-tale life with a big house, garden and white picket fence. God is full of surprises.

Although I could see my husband's calling, I did not know mine. It took me eighteen years on the mission field before I realized my own. Sometimes we move ahead in faith, unsure. Seeing purpose as more of a responsibility than a high call from God, we forge ahead, believing God just might want to use us, as is, even with faults and frailties.

When I was in my early thirties and my children were little, my calling looked different than it does now. Washing dirty diapers by hand was not a favorite part of my early vocation. But in all the stages of life, we have calling and responsibility. Perhaps we need to stop looking for the burning bush experience and ask a different question. Instead of wondering, '*Is God calling me?*,' maybe the question should be '*Why not? Why wouldn't God be calling me?*'

When it comes to calling, we have high and lofty expectations. Gideon, Paul, Mary, Noah. Matthew, Mark, Luke, John. But God calls us to add our own names to the list. Rakoto, Nolavy, Patsy, Eduardo.

Ninety percent of American missionaries don't make it through the first three-year term. Some friends and family members didn't think we would either. Some supporters shared their impression:

> *We remember when you both came to visit. There you were sitting on our couch with your two small children, like any other young married couple, telling us your dreams and ambitions in life. You were going to serve as missionaries in Madagascar but didn't know much about the country, had never been there and didn't even know where it was located except because of the game Risk. When you left, my wife and I looked at each other and said, "They'll never make it."*

Are you Willing?

On my 43rd birthday I woke up from a dream. Short, clear and concise, I was called to become a priest.

Later that morning, driving on a bumpy road near Tamatave, Madagascar, to participate in a seminar with Todd, I broached the subject, expecting disagreement.

"Honey, I had a dream that I was supposed to become a priest."

Thinking for a moment, he responded. *"Yes. I think so."*

Rats. I thought the dream was stupid.

The power of God and the Holy Spirit will allow us to do more than we could ever want or imagine. God's Call is bigger than ourselves.

Sometimes the question of considering our calling is simple. Instead of searching for the burning bush, maybe God is just asking, "Are you willing?"

Again, let's look at Gideon. What made him so successful? Although he was just one, he did not go alone. Drawing help from all ethnic groups, he worked together and united people. As a man of faith[30] he talked with God, often. He had a talkative soul. Radical change takes radical prayer. We need a talkative soul.

> Radical prayer goes to the root, the heart, the center. The word radical itself comes from the Latin *radiz*, which means root. Radical prayer refuses to let us

stay on the fringes of life's great issues. It dares to believe that things can be different. Its' aim is the total transformation of persons, institutions, and societies. Radical prayer, you see, is prophetic.[31]

God calls us to pray for the rising up of a new generation of leaders, "prophets of the apostolic mold."[32] Leaders who gather the people of God into communities of radical faithfulness are called into fresh, bold expressions of faithfulness and obedience. Perhaps we ourselves are an answer to our own prayer!

Stepping into Our Calling

It might not be easy, but eventually we all have to step into our calling. When we were still living at St. Julian's Center in Redhill, Kenya, we received an email from Bishop Remi, Bishop of Madagascar and Archbishop of the Province of the Indian Ocean. Contacting Todd about his upcoming consecration as Bishop of Toliara, Archbishop Remi told Todd that he must speak with his wife about the issue of women's ordination since the Province of the Indian Ocean didn't (yet) ordain women. And my ordination into the priesthood was just nine days away!

I struggled. Even though I would become ordained into the priesthood, I am not a churchy person. I prefer to find God in a garden or on a golf course rather than with a lot of pomp and circumstance. But my day of ordination on September 3rd, 2006 was something special. In a way, it was like getting married to the Lord.

I had been meditating on Malachi 2:2, 6-7.

> Set your heart to honor me. True instruction was in [her] mouth and nothing false was found on [her] lips. [She] walked with me in peace and uprightness and turned many from sin. For the lips of a priest are to preserve knowledge and from their mouth people should seek instruction because [she] is the messenger of the Lord Almighty.

As I walked into my calling my prayer was steadfast. *Lord, help me to be a priest who has set my heart to honor you!*

A friend wrote an email of jubilation on my day of ordination. "I don't know what it means to have your bishop be your husband, but I'm sure you'll figure out how to support each other vocationally."

Leadership for all. Men, women, even children. Valuing simplicity of life and equality of all in the eyes of God, the Celtic church encouraged leadership for everyone. Women were valued and not ignored. Women leaders held powerful ecclesial positions and headed monastic communities. One of the reasons the Diocesan Cathedral was called St. Patrick is because of this Celtic approach to Christianity.[33]

At times it was excruciating to live out my calling as a woman priest in a country that did not yet fully agree on women's ordination. I spent more than my share of tearing up in the pew, fighting the urge not to cry or shout, just because I was a woman. My heart wanted to serve. I didn't want to quench the spirit of God within. I wanted to fulfill my calling. By the grace of God, I did. And to the glory of God, other women are courageously following.

Sometimes living out our calling can be like swimming upstream in a downstream world. But we are called to persevere, no matter the circumstances of life.

God's Call in Large and Small Ways

More may be asked of us than we think. We offer what we have. Our call could also be simpler than we realize. This is the mystery of God's plan. Even when unsure, we trust God step by step.

Four simple guidelines remind us that calling doesn't have to be complicated. Sometimes, we just start where we are, in our present situation.

1) Awareness of need. Certainly, there was need in Madagascar. I still call it the forgotten island. What is the awareness of need near you?

2) Who is calling? Are we listening?

3 Why not? When we believe we have a calling, the calling will be tested. Put it in the positive. Why wouldn't God call me?

4) Obedience. Will we follow?

There is power in just one person following their call. The Lord looked for just one person who would be willing to build up the wall and stand before God in the gap on behalf of the land... but he found no one.[34] Will he find you?

One day, God found me in the kitchen after a meal.

Goop and glob after baking the turkey left a hard impossible-to-clean crust on the pan. Stuck, it needed to soak. But that's not what *I* wanted to do. I wanted to finish cleaning the kitchen. Believing that was my responsibility after Todd cooked the turkey, I wanted every pan finished so the kitchen was organized. And yet the pan needed to soak. *I, I, I.* Finally admitting applying more elbow grease would not suffice, I surrendered and let it soak to loosen up the grub and grime.

After cooking four eggs over easy, I returned to the sink. Stacking the dishes to the left, I prepared two blue plastic tubs, one for soaking and washing, the other bleaching and rinsing. In the routine of soapy bubbles, I found a calling. The call was to be in the moment.

As the pan soaked in bubbles, I soaked in thought. Sometimes, we are also called to soak, in character, preparing for the future. With not a scrap wasted, God uses all our situations. Jesus healed a man with just spit and dirt, promising life abundantly. When the Holy Spirit lives within us in the simplicity of life as our Constant Companion, Comforter and Counselor, he calls, every moment of every day. Are we listening?

"I am only one; but still, I am one. I cannot do everything; but still, I can do something. I will not refuse to do the something I can do."[35] Sometimes it takes a blind person to point out true perspective. Many attribute this quote to Helen Keller. Indeed, she quoted it often and called upon it for strength throughout her life. But, it originated with the Rev. Edward Hale who met Helen when she was eight years old and their relationship continued for twenty years until his death. This has also become the motto of the Daughters of the King of the Episcopal Church.

Mother Teresa followed the same principle. Trusting God, we are called to soak in the present moment, in God's softening love, and to pass this love on, person-to-person, heart-to-heart. "If you can't feed a hundred people, then feed just one."[36] As we soak, we do what we can, finding God's call in large and small ways.

A Smile is the Beginning of Love

Climbing the cement stairs to our compact apartment, I wondered how I would ever withstand life in Toliara. Everything was altered. Gone were the lovely gardens of Limuru, Kenya, where everything flourished and thrived. Stark reality brought hovels, holes and a myriad of mysteries. Now, residing in the spiny desert, everything seemed like thorns in my flesh.

Her smile changed my life. As new neighbors, Nolavy and I had never met, but she was glad to see me. Living in a small tin hut next-door, her living space housed seventeen people including grandfather, cousins and small babies. Her father, the *Shaman*, was a well-known, strong leader in the community. Cultures and skin color vastly in contrast, God called us to be neighbors.

"Let us always meet each other with a smile, for the smile is the beginning of love."[37]

Mother Teresa is one of my models of a woman living out her call. Founding the order of Missionaries of Charity in 1950, her lifestyle of love to the poorest of the poor in India began as she "felt called by the people's sufferings." Due to Mother Teresa's "call within a call" she left the comfort of the convent of Loreto and set her mind to help the poor and live among them. In determining which work would be done, there was no planning at all. "I heeded the work in accordance to how I felt called by the people's sufferings. God made me see what he wanted me to do."[38]

Did you catch that? I think it bears repeating. "God made me see what he wanted me to do." Are we sensitive enough to the Spirit of God so that He helps us to see what He wants us to do?

Mother Teresa quite simply chose to leave the life of the convent and live among the people she served. Her example of indigenous communal life breaks down walls and barriers. Inspiring me, especially on the hard days, her words brought wisdom and a purpose of relational evangelism with a spirit of love, prayer, education, discipleship and evangelism.

This lifestyle of evangelism and disciple-making caused us to be intentional in building community at the Cathedral Complex. Intentionally living side by side reminded me to make relationships with others because faith stems from relational connections. When mission is about the product or outcome, community gets pushed aside and the purpose remains rootless. In order to understand how to reach a community, a person has to become a part of it. This can demand a level of discomfort. Getting out of our easy chair, we endure stress while living in uncomfortable situations. A comfort zone may be a beautiful place, but it's doubtful that anything grows there.

Stretching out a hand, and being willing to be led into new neighborhoods of our calling takes courage. In a blind trust-walk, we walk a craggy mountain path. If we stumble and fall, God will catch us. Every calling has conflict. No matter the situation, let's remember Mother Teresa's wisdom and always greet one another with a smile, for the smile is the beginning of love.

Strategic Living

Basically, as Todd and I lived out our callings, we focused on three things:

1) Pray. God is the center.
2) Observe what God is doing, and do that.
3) Make disciples. Build relationships.

When Todd was called to Toliara to strategically begin a new diocese in 2006, my younger daughter Charese (17) and I were still in Kenya and our older daughter Corbi (18) began college in the USA. My unassuming bishop-husband concentrated on living among the people, building relationships. Living in a small room with a young Malagasy, Todd ventured into new territory by *pusse-pusse* (rickshaw.)

When I joined him several months later, we lived locally, in the very crowded neighborhood of Ankilifaly and our priority remained to form friendships. The small second floor apartment overlooked tin hovels, stick huts and pit latrines.

Without a surrounding wall, the uncompleted church building became the center for the community.

Pioneering in an area the size of France, my husband was determined to live like the people. When we traveled within the diocese, we stayed overnight with clergy and parishioners, in their homes. God does his work through people, through you and through me. With God at the center, we build relationships and pray together. We observe what God is doing, and jump on board with him.

We also planned and strategized for the future. Todd put systems and structure into place. We raised money for a Diocesan Center including St. Patrick's Cathedral, Diocesan offices, residences, an educational center, and St. Patrick's Anglican Bible School. Economic development became a priority. Since 90% of the parishioners in the south earned less than $1 a day, we focused on holistic ministry. A Master Plan for the Cathedral Complex was analyzed with a team. Plans were drawn up by a professional architect who lived in the USA and yet came the long distance to be on-sight and visit the land. We used local contractors. A few years later the Women's Center was dedicated and the Children's Educational Sponsorship Program began. All these efforts and more were carefully planned to help transform lives of impoverished Malagasy caught in the cycle of poverty.

As we lived with the people and strategized for the future, we focused on leadership development. From the beginning, building relationships and discipleship were priorities. Pinpointing future Malagasy leaders, we began partnerships with Downline Ministries and Rooted in Jesus. We emphasized the 4 Cs of leadership - Calling, Character, Chemistry and Competency - which, sandwiched in by Courage and Community, outline the structure of this book.

One Lenten season I studied Henri Nouwen's *Can You Drink the Cup?* Reminded that we all have a cup to hold, carry, drink, and offer to others, each call is unique. Wisely Nouwen writes:

> No two lives are the same. We often compare our lives with those of others, trying to decide if we are better or worse off, but such comparisons do not help us much. We have to live our life, not someone else's. We have to hold our own cup. We have to dare say: "This is my life, the life that is given to me, and it is this life that I have to live as well as I can. My life is unique. Nobody else will ever live it. I have my own history, my own family, my own body, my own character, my own friends, my own way of thinking, speaking and acting – yes, I have my own life to live. No one else has the same challenge. I am alone because I am unique. Many people can help me live my life, but after all is said and done, I have to make my own choices about how to live.[39]

God has called each one of us. Our callings are unique. How do you live into your calling? How do you hold your own cup?

"I Always Wanted To Be A Good Dad"

Just like I didn't realize what our call to Madagascar would entail, I didn't fully realize caring for my father just before his death was also a step in my calling and would require abundance of stamina and strength. I guess I thought death was a bit like checking off a task – finished, done. I know that sounds cold and cruel, but I had never experienced a close, intimate, loved one dying before.

When Dad began his steady physical decline in 2019, mom and I hoped to skip the crisis. Having been diagnosed years earlier with lung cancer, we knew death was on the doorstep. We thought we were prepared and now prayed that Dad would go quickly, without pain. I guess we wanted to skip the hard stuff and rest in the outcome - knowing Dad was in heaven. But that was too lofty an expectation. Every death has crisis. Every calling has conflict.

Dad and I were resting on Mom and Dad's king size bed, aware that his days on earth were shortening quickly. We held hands; tears streaming down our cheeks. Expressing love to one another, we blessed one another, giving gratitude to God for making us family. The DNA was aligned exactly in a way that out of all the billions of people on earth, he and I would be father and daughter.

"I always wanted to be a good dad," he said with tears. That was dad's call, and he accomplished it with pride. Absorbing his words, more thoughts came to mind. *Perfect love casts out all fear.*[40]

On his deathbed, there was no longer fear of mistakes. Hungry for love, we experienced compassion hand in hand. Celebratory were moments of perfect love between imperfect people because we know a perfect God.

Perfect. This definition brings depth of meaning from the Greek translation. Perfect does not mean without fault nor mistake, but rather complete, *whole*.

Transition of life on earth to life eternal is a challenging time. Doubts, insecurities, wanderings, walk us to places we can only go to with Jesus. God takes us into the deep. In order to be truly effective for God, we learn to humble ourselves, following God with simple trust and obedience.

Some people look for a beautiful life. Others make life beautiful. Following our calling makes life beautiful.

Thin Space

One of the reasons I love the Malagasy culture is they live in thin space – the space where heaven and earth meet and is paper thin. The Malagasy people know life is a gift. With an average lifespan of 56 years, they do not feel entitled to live a long life. Life is a gift to live together. God numbers our days.

Living in the present moment allows this awareness and thin space. Our lives are in God's hand, and sometimes the call is very simple. Live a grateful life. Greet one another with a smile. Spread love. And like Dad, remember your purpose in life.

What vocation ought to be mine? The one that awakens my soul. Whatever our calling, it is bigger than ourselves, because it causes dependence on God. Scottish novelist Robert Louis Stevenson wrote, "There is no duty we so much underrate as the duty of being happy."

Work for God cannot be separated and contained into little waffle-like boxes. It is mixed up like spaghetti, messy and all encompassing. Whatever we *do* is secondary. Our call is to be happy.

In Madagascar, I loved my work as I helped develop crafts to help transform women's lives, fighting for a better standard of living empowering them to feed their families and educate their children. Laying hands on the infected and shaking the stub of a one-armed man stretched my comfort zone, giving deep satisfaction. I learned to rejoice in abundant life as people were set free and delivered, all to the glory of God. Life is bigger than we are.

Smiling to our neighbor, we live in thin space, even while here on earth. Rejoice always. Pray constantly. Give thanks to God in all circumstances. This calling will have a ripple effect through the whole community.

Have we forgotten the simple call of just being happy? Instead of checking off To-Do Lists and focusing on productivity, we celebrate God and scatter joy in the midst of whatever we are doing. Enjoy God and the world in which we live is a simple call, and yet it is lost in many cultures of today's modern world. Maybe this simple calling is truly the heart of the gospel, loving God and loving our neighbors as ourselves. ...And never underestimate the value of a smile. It might change someone's life.

Blessed

Many global workers become burnt out, overworked, fatigued and shattered. I had. Was I over-striving to live out my calling?

Forgetting our unique gifts and talents and comparing our-selves with one another lays a snare, a dangerous trap for thinking our acceptance comes through what we do for God rather than in our relationship with God.

> Dr. Frank Lake specialized in working with missionaries who had become exhausted or bitter in their work. After countless interviews, he concluded that the problem for many of these people was that they were trying to use their work to achieve acceptance – to prove their worth to God, others, and themselves. Lake argued that we can only do healthy, sustainable work when we are operating from acceptance – when we realize there is nothing we can do to make God love us more and nothing we can do to make God love us less.[41]

The Greek word for happy is *makarios.* Taken from the Vulgate or Latin version word *beatitudo* in Matthew's Gospel this word refers to the Beatitudes and the Sermon on the Mount.[42] Happy are they that know their need for God, for they shall be sat-isfied. Deep joy is serene, secure, completely independent of all situations and is dependent on our relationship with God alone.

It is this permeating joy of life that the Malagasy have given us in return for our service to them. This perspective, this blessedness, is joy that shines through tears. Profound joy is unshakable, not taken away in challenging circumstances. The Malagasy people live in the context of suffering and yet live with joy in the present moment. Humbly admitting their poverty, they are not hero people but articulate the lifestyle of community and utter dependence on God. They live in a blessed state.[43]

The Joyful Call to Worship

Each day we have a calling. Starting with little steps, how do we fulfill that calling? Choosing joy, abundant life in Christ and blessings is part of that calling, called to bless and be blessed. Most of all, we trust God, gather friends and pray.

While living in the shanty borough of Ankilifaly between November 2007 and December 2011, I was frustrated because I couldn't have a potted plant. If I had one outside on the staircase, it would be stolen or crushed and soil toppled over our doorstep. Unsatisfied and irritated, I wanted to see beauty. From each of our six windows there were neighboring pit latrines with corresponding smells wafting into our apartment. This was certainly not my definition of beauty. So, I began to pray in color.

On our last home visit, a friend had given me Sybil McBeth's book, *Praying In Color*.[44] The author was also the wife of an Episcopal priest, as was my friend Sherry, who gave me the gift saying, "Patsy, I think you would like this book." I chuckled to myself noticing the creativity in the idea of keeping interested in praying while living a lifetime sitting in the church pew as your husband preaches.

With Sharpie markers and index cards, we sat on the unfinished concrete step to the church, played a worship music CD and doodled. People of the village walked by with their straw mats on their way to sleep under the large shade tree which had become their local resting spot. Curious, they would hear the music and stop. Greeting one another, we would invite them to join us. Handing them paper and marker, a number of them would put down their mats and participate.

People gathered to doodle and color and prayers were being answered! Prayers were filed in index boxes and these boxes metaphorically became potted plants – a community prayer garden of seeds soon to become beautiful flowers rewarding a bountiful harvest, fertilized with God's love and watered by the neighborhood. Many of these index cards and prayers have been kept and filed in the diocesan history books to remind us all that the Diocese of Toliara was founded in prayer.

Happy are those who hear the joyful call of worship, for they will walk in the light of God's Presence.[45] Those who hear (and heed) the joyful call of worship and praying in color, even on their way to take a nap, will rejoice all day long.

Now that's my type of calling!

Opportunities for Personal Reflection

"The hand of God has been upon you, wooing you, winning you, drawing you to himself."[46] True, abundant life in Christ comprises a radical way of living. Do you feel a nudge from the Lord prompting you to embrace your call today?

Four simple guidelines remind us that calling doesn't have to be complicated. Sometimes, we just start where we are, in our present situation. How can you apply these four guidelines to your own life?

1) Awareness of need. What is the awareness of need near you?

2) Who is calling? Are you listening?

3) Why not? When we believe we have a calling, the calling will be tested. Put it in the positive. Why wouldn't God call me?

4) Obedience. Will you follow?

Chapter Three

CHARACTER

Happy are those who remain faithful under trials,
because when they succeed in passing such a test,
they will receive as their reward the life that God
has promised to those who love him.
James 1:12

Glad-to-See-You-Joy!

Waking up at 3:00 am and walking 35 km, it took hours to find water. Finally, arriving at the village town supplied with a small amount, there was already a long line at the only tap in town. Marolahy waited in line 12 hours and finally paid a day's wages (about 80 cents) for 20 liters of water of questionable quality. And then, after all hours of daylight had been spent waiting in the scorching sun, he carried the 20 liter container of water back to his village, alternating positions on his back and his head.

But he didn't do this alone. He endured this hardship with friends. Not entitled to anything else except dependency on God, earth and fellow mankind, comrades walked miles together searching for firewood or fetching water. In their daily lifestyle, the Malagasy establish community and joy.

Malagasy people are some of the happiest people I know. Astonished and amazed at their joy amidst adversities, curious foreigners visiting Madagascar wonder why. With so many hardships in life, how do the Malagasy people, their lives overshadowed by extreme poverty, the most primitive of living conditions, lack of schools and health care, remain so full of joy?

There is a neurological reason for happiness. Brain development explains that the joy center exists in the right orbital prefrontal cortex of the brain.[47] When joy is sufficiently developed, it regulates emotion, pain control and immunity centers and has executive control to override the entire emotional system. Joy is produced when someone is glad-to-see-you.[48] Living in multigenerational, family-oriented communities, the Malagasy people have deep connection with one another through relationships.

When first moving to Toliara, our compact apartment was too small to fit the refrigerator. Whenever I wanted a cold drink (and Toliara was hot!) I walked out of the house, down the stairs overlooking our neighbor's tin dwelling and entered another person's living space to finally find the room containing the refrigerator., At the start, this infuriated me! What a great inconvenience! But over time I came to see it as an opportunity.

Nolavy's smile and glad-to-see-you morning greeting gave me energy. Love and friendship formed around a desire to be together. Each morning I soon looked forward to seeing her smile. It brought me joy and happiness. Genuinely desiring to spend time together, we sang, prayed-in-color, read the Bible and walked the city of Toliara, beseeching God's blessings. Love motivates and liberates us to become our full selves.

According to brain research, joy is this foundation for the development of all other maturity and growth. Most parts of the brain stop continuing to develop, but the joy center never loses capacity to grow. This specific part of the brain grows in response to joy-filled, authentic relationships.

The image of Nolavy's smiling face on that hot November day over a decade ago still returns me to joy. Picturing her beautiful smile, joy unshackles me, reminding me to live in truth, closeness, joy and peace. As neighbors, Nolavy's family became a blessing. Becoming friends, her father, Remamy, the local shaman, promised us protection from gunfire and thievery during a political coup. As mentioned in the Introduction, he eventually surrendered all spiritual authority for Nolavy's future as a leader in the church to my husband and me and she became the first woman ordained as an Anglican priest in the Diocese of Toliara.

And how did it all begin? With a prayer, a morning greeting, a happy-to-see-you smile and loving one's neighbor as one's self.

Humility

Everywhere in the world, people are hungry. Thirsty for spiritual truth, fervent prayer takes hard work, humility and turning around in one's spiritual life.

Working with the poor in Madagascar, I have found that many people do not first ask for bread or clothing, but for a Bible. God has created each one of us with an ingrained desire for the truth and to know Him intimately. Hungering and thirsting after righteousness and soaking ourselves in the Word of God is necessary for all of us in the world today.

The *ombiasy*, the Malagasy name for witchdoctor derives its meaning from *olona-be-hasina,* or 'person of much virtue.' There is a Malagasy proverb, 'Man can do nothing to alter his destiny,' but the *mpanandro* (astrologer) will advise on the best day to build a house, or hold a wedding or *famadihana* (turning of the ancestors bones.) The Malagasy have a deep knowledge of herbal medicine and the market just next to the church displayed a variety of medicinal plants, amulets and talismans. It is not uncommon to see Malagasy wear charms or use local medicines to ward off evil spirits. When moving to the south, the medical doctor even suggested to our house helper that she burn her monthly personal hygiene remnants because the witchdoctors may go to the local trash dump and remove objects, using them in their witchcraft session.

Some of the greatest barriers to sharing the gospel are social and cultural. Active, loving engagement, observing thought patterns, understanding world-views, listening to questions, and feeling burdens forms the basis for the development of relationships and informs thoughtful responses to needs. Humility is especially helpful when bridging the cultural gap and hosting mission teams and working with diverse groups of people. However different the group background, love is the open door to friendship. Relational evangelism is the keystone for people of diverse backgrounds to partner together. Humbly being with one another allows a constant interchange of 'learning and doing' and the ongoing dialogue helps foster relationships with one another.

Jesus enjoyed being with seekers far more than being with religious leaders, and people enjoyed being with Jesus. Love and humility are key character traits for church planting and church growth, wherever in the world the Lord might lead us. Our job is to make the gospel culturally sensitive to the local people, building Christians who will carry on the task of making disciples in the years to come. Building the next generation of leaders through loving one another - the Great Commandment - is what evangelism - the Great Commission - is all about.

Soaking Prayer

Learning to cook with only a few simple ingredients, I was preparing *loka*, the side dish to the rice the Malagasy eat three times a day. Basic cooking creativity led me to decide upon small beans, somewhat like a tiny lentil. Mixed with potatoes, tomatoes, onion and a bouillon cube, perhaps it could become a decent dish upon the dinner table. The beans began cooking at 2:00 pm and continued throughout the afternoon.

Four hours later the beans still clung to the side of the pot as hard as marbles upon a wood floor. Discouraged and disheartened, I left my house and went to talk to our neighbor. Laughing, I exclaimed, "*Mahandro aho, fa tsy misy masaka.*" (*I cook, but nothing is ready to eat.*) Chuckling at my cooking catastrophe, she explained—first, the beans must soak in water.

Humility soaks situations in prayer. It is a great temptation to do the work of the Lord with energy and gumption. However, if we activate without soaking prayer, we may spin wheels for God with great momentum, but without going anywhere.

"If my people, who are called by my name will humble themselves and pray, seek my face and turn from their wicked ways, I will hear from heaven and will forgive their sins and restore their land."[49] The Lord spoke these words to Solomon after he had finished building the temple of the Lord and the royal palace. Solomon had succeeded in carrying out all he had in mind to do.

Soaking prayer and marinating in the Word of God, is like tilling the soil, preparing the ground for planting. Where is the most unique place you have ever prayed? Recently, as I now live in the USA, I prayed with a woman in a swimming pool. Tears rolled down her face as she shared a tragic experience. With character of humility, spending time with God in soaking prayer, softens us to hearing him, following him and sharing his heart with others, all to the glory of God.

Holy Fragility

Bumping down the dirt trek we stopped and parked the gray Ford pickup as the brush thickened. Our legs would have to take us the rest of the way. Running to greet us, crowds kissed my hand and my husband's bishop-ring, joyfully escorting us to the far end of the village. They were excited to show us the areas where water tanks had been strategically placed to capture the long-hoped-for rain water during the upcoming, short rainy season. Conversation took place in several dialects. Although we could not understand their local dialect, we spoke in the official language. Communication was humbly adequate.

Life is fragile; nearly eighty percent of the Malagasy live in extreme poverty. Stick houses, dirt floors and palm thatch roofs are the norm. According to UNICEF, out of 100 children entering primary school, only eight children finish the equivalent of 9th grade in the U.S. system.

With a life expectancy rate of only 56 years, their deep fragility establishes humility. With dependency upon God and their community, life is not to be lived independently. Dependent upon the land for cooking, bathing and daily living brings heightened awareness of God's resources. Weakness becomes strength. Dependence on God guides the day. Joy blossoms and a vibrant spiritual garden begins to flourish.

I am most happy then, to be proud of my weaknesses, in order to feel the protection of Christ's power over me.[50] Paul reminds me to be content with weaknesses, insults, hardships, persecutions, and difficulties for Christ's sake. For when I am weak, then I am strong! We fall, but we get up. We may limp, but we move forward.

Research finds that joy levels increase in an environment of humility with other's responding warmly to weakness.[51] Anticipating a comforting response from others for our weakness allows us freedom to search and find help quickly. When problems are hidden to avoid feeling shamed, they soon escalate out of fear of revealing our vulnerability.

Blessed with humility, the Malagasy realize they are not in control of this life. Unlike the western world, clothes and wealth are not the focus of life. Believing everything truly needed is provided for, or not, by *Zanahary*, the God of their ancestors, the Malagasy develop deep trust in God. Humble in heart, this trust in God creates a blessedness of life.

Spirituality becomes holy living, every moment precious with God. Protected by God and living with others offers an atmosphere of *sambatra* – happy, blessed - even during difficulty. As a family-oriented society, decisions are made based on relationships, family and community. With humility and tenderness there is a deep tolerance of one another... A person is complimented for being *tsotra* - simple, easy to get along with.

Taking our hands in theirs at the end of the day, the Malagasy from the village hoping for water tanks escorted us back to our vehicle. As I slipped into the passenger's seat, an elderly woman glanced at the side view mirror. Never seeing her reflection in a mirror before, she grinned from ear to ear. "Oh, that's what I look like."

Maybe this is a key to selfless living. Not worrying about the looking glass, or even recognizing our own reflection in the mirror. It's the community that matters and our humble participation in what the world offers us. Satisfying humility combined with gratitude blossom living in the moment with total dependence on God. Humility knows holy fragility is part of being human. And like the village woman surprised by her reflection in the side view car mirror, we pleasantly exclaim, "Oh, that's what I look like!"

Sugar-Water- Sweet-Hospitality

Cheerful voices broke open like floodgates, villagers bursting forth, spilling greetings with tooth-gapped smiles. Elders limped along using sticks as canes. Children ran ahead tumbling over one another with laughter and joy.

Sweating profusely and blisters on our feet from the two-hour trek, we were gratefully escorted into the church building. Sitting on a 2'x4' piece of plywood built as a church pew, we rested in the first permanent church structure for the Malagasy Episcopal Church in the southern area of Madagascar. St Joseph's Church in Boynton Beach, Florida had blessed the Diocese, donating funds to build a sister church in the rural village of Betaola. The villagers were ecstatic.

After prayers, teachings and presentations in the church, we walked through the dusty hamlet. Proudly, the church president spoke of their new breeding program, cattle purchased with a financial donation from St. Joseph's Church in America. After hearing stories of celebration and thanksgiving for this new program, we were asked to join the church president in his home.

Sitting on small stools just inches above the ground, we crouched in a tiny dark hut with only a few rays of light slipping through the single window. This family was considered wealthy. Their double bed with floppy mattress would sleep seven. Others in the homestead crowded together sleeping on straw mats. Gifted with hospitality, this loving family offered what they had in their humble abode. Today it was sugar and boiled water. Sipping sweetness, I absorbed love and generosity.

Anybody who comes to a Malagasy home is considered a gift from God. Visitors stopping in are like angels unawares. Taking care of guests is highly respected and admired. Many times a *kabary* is exchanged, mutual words of blessing expressed to wish another well, provisions to be returned in blessing one another. With a sense of unity, their kindness, generosity and hospitality will someday be passed on to another. It's not what they serve that is important, it is how they serve it. Sugar-water-sweet-hospitality served from the heart doesn't focus on what they don't have, it shares what that family does have.

Years later, I was in conversation with a girl studying for her high school diploma. Asking for prayer, she told me a bit about her background. "Neny Patsy, I am from Betaola. I am the church president's daughter."

And then the brain light bulb switched on. *Oh my! She was the young child in the dark room, whose face I could barely see except for the small ray of light shining from the window. Her family was the one who served us sugar-water-sweet-hospitality!*

Henri Nouwen writes of "hospitality of the heart." Hospitality at its core is the opening of the heart. Opening our hearts means gathering others in.[52] Because of this philosophy of opening our hearts to one another, we named the Diocesan Offices and Bishop's Residence, *Ny Trano Fihaonana*, The Gathering Place, when we moved there in December 2011. This may be more difficult when those to whom we open our hearts are quite diverse in nature. It takes particular courage to fully open our hearts to strangers and those who are as different from us as a giraffe is from a rhinoceros. Yet by doing so, we are blessed.

Sugar-water-sweet hospitality begins with welcoming one another into this world, blessing one another with kindness. Sugar-water-sweet smiles of welcome with open arms bless others before they know we are coming their way.

Four Toes and a Gash

Three men came closer. One was limping, using a stick for a cane. Stopping me on the dusty road, he begged. "*Azafady. Mila vavaka aho.*" Please, I need prayer. Pointing to his foot, there was one toe missing and a huge gash. An indentation in the arch, half the size of a tennis ball, was gouged out of his left foot.

The wound looked calloused. Without access to health care nor a few dollars to go to a clinic, I wondered how long the man's foot had been diseased. I felt like Peter. "Silver and gold have I none, but what I do have, I give thee."[53] On that morning walk, I was not carrying coins in my pocket, but we always have a prayer.

His words were different than "please pray for me." "Please, I need prayer." Begging, humble, total transparency with total trust, his soul was laid bare. There was an underlying expectation of a generous response. He was asking, "Help!"

I extended my arm and my hand and in Malagasy prayed for him for healing and to experience the love of Christ and blessed him. In gratitude, he gave thanks.

Broken, fallen, weak and vulnerable, human beings are unable to avoid difficult circumstances. Loving communities help encourage and accompany us on our road to recovery and wholeness. Responding tenderly to weakness is one of the Malagasy people's greatest strengths. A community intended to connect people to one another in loving relationships results in helping each person discover who they are. People need people.

Amidst living a communal lifestyle, I believe the majority of the Malagasy people live in a state of happiness, being blessed, because together, they recognize their need for God. The Malagasy version of the Beatitudes reads, *Blessed are they who realize their need for God...*

This idea of poor in spirit portrays realization of our utter helplessness and the need to put our whole trust in God. Addressing to the community, Jesus speaks as if to articulate the lifestyle of those who know that the only way life is going to be lived is in utter dependence on God. This is the blessed state.[54]

No doubt, the Malagasy realize their need for God. It's not usually thought that meekness, hunger and persecution can be associated with blessedness. But being blessed is not the reward of our faith endeavors but rather with knowing our need for God. Jesus speaks these Beatitudes, this blessedness, in the context of hardship and suffering. The blessedness of this very moment is because God is with us everywhere, anytime, in all circumstances.

Recognizing a total need for God is a reminder that we live above our conditions, having a joy for living no matter what our surroundings. God chose the poor people of this world to be rich in faith and to possess the kingdom, which he promised to those who love him.[55]

Tipping-the-Hat-Kindness

Walking in the spiny desert with flip flops and cane, an elderly gentleman paused to greet us, tipping his hat with a slight bow.

Sweetly stirred at this gentlemanly gesture, and me a romantic at heart, I asked my husband rambling by my side. *"Todd, did you notice that? He tipped his hat!"*

Always ready with a quip, Todd responded, *"I thought he dropped it!"*

With a slight chuckle the sandy trek became a sacred path, engulfed in warmth and kindness. Madagascar, where I have lived for almost three decades, is a place that gives me insight to the sacred world. From the Malagasy, I have learned to be a giver and a receiver.

Turning on the light for those in the world around me, they have taught me the importance of allowing others to hold the lamp for me as we walk the path of life together. Used by God, the Red Island has been a fueling station of energy and purpose.

"Too often we underestimate the power of a touch, a smile, a kind word, a listening ear, an honest compliment, or the smallest act of caring, all of which have the potential to turn a life around."[56] Small things, like a kind gesture of tipping a hat, teach us how to handle big things. Actions may speak louder than words, leaving a healing touch, a gentle whisper of love and kindness.

Later, I was walking with a missionary friend who assists in translation of the Bible, and I shared this story. Bev mentioned that the Tesaka ethnic group's term for worship, is literally translated, "to take off one's hat." A Bible translator for years, she continued to explain, "I know, it sounds really inappropriate, but they absolutely insist. Tipping one's hat is a very serious thing for them; an expression of the utmost respect and honor."

Here's an example. Luke 4:8 in Tesaka: *Da hoy e navaliny: Vasoratry: 'F e Jañahary ñe hipoahanao satroky, Ijy koa ñe hotopoinao.* (Jesus answered: "It is written: 'It is God you will/ must worship (lit. take your hats off to), him you will/must serve as master.'")[57]

What if we had the vision to see every person in our life as someone to serve, someone to whom we 'tip our hat'? What if our first response was the desire to be kind, to be of service the way Jesus was?

Breastfeeding and Bike Riding

Amazingly, I've even seen mothers breastfeeding at the oddest times; riding on the back of a bicycle, in an ox-cart, washing clothes and even while balancing a bucket on top of her head! I consider this astonishing multitasking!

Designed to constantly give nourishment to her child, a kind mother is a life-giver to her family. Kindness also gives life to others through service and by obeying Jesus model of loving one another just as he has loved us. I wonder, what is the most effective way to be a person who blesses, loves and gives nourishment to others?

Now I live in a land of golf carts and swimming pools. No longer thatched roof single-room huts, here homes are large with four bedrooms and boats docked in the canal. We bless animals and have a special service for dogs and cats. Pets are walked in strollers, welcomed in restaurants and travel with their owners on airplanes. Decorations for Halloween are as plentiful as for Christmas. I am feeling the pull of cultural differences.

And yet interactions of life are made with intention to serve, to give of ourselves and make our homes and communities a better place. Do you want days to matter and moments to be memorable? God needs our smile in this world. God needs our kind words and love for one another to create beauty upon this earth. God needs us to be his blessing wherever we are!

What If?
What if...I really trusted these words – "Fear not, for I am with you."
What if...I really believed this statement – "Be not dismayed, for I am your God."
What if...I woke up in the morning with first thoughts – "I will strengthen you, Yes, I will help you."
What if...I continued realizing through the day that God is "upholding me with His righteous right hand."[58]

Would I?
Would I...be less anxious? More at peace?
Would I...be more confident? Less doubtful of myself?
Would I...be different? Viewing life from a different lens?
Would I...be more gentle with myself and with others?

"God is more anxious to bestow His blessings on us than we are to receive them. One loving soul sets another on fire."[59] Passing on blessings and love to one another is part of our God-created role in life.

Celebrate!

"From the moment you close your Bible in the morning, nearly everything else you'll encounter throughout the day will be luring you away from its truths. The opinions of your coworkers, the news coverage on television, your typical web sites, the various temptations of the day – all of these and more will be working overtime to shape your perceptions of what's true and most desirable in life."[60]

Many things will be said so loudly and frequently that if we are not careful, we can start believing them. But the real meaning of life deepens in the Word. The Scriptures are more than good principles. They are instructions guiding us to the only pathway to real blessing. When we observe people with depth of character grow in godliness, we rejoice.

"There is no greater joy than to see my children walking in the truth."[61] Love rejoices in the things that please God. When our friends and family are growing in Christian character, we have reason to celebrate. We cheer others on for allowing God to accomplish great things in their lives.

> We ought always to give thanks to God for you, brethren, as is only fitting, because your faith is greatly enlarged, and the love of each one of you toward one another grows ever greater; therefore, we ourselves speak proudly of you among the churches of God for your perseverance and faith in the midst of all your persecutions and afflictions which you endure.[62]

Celebrate during the process of growth in Christian character.

Celebrate walking in the truth.

Celebrate God accomplishing great things in our life.

Celebrate life with a happy–to–see–you smile and a heart filled with love.

Opportunities for Personal Reflection

Character

The Power of One[63]

One song can spark a moment, One whisper
can wake the dream.
One tree can start a forest, One bird can herald spring.

One smile begins a friendship, One moment
can make one fall in love.
One star can guide a ship at sea, One word
can frame the goal.

One vote can change a nation, One sunbeam
lights a room.
One candle wipes out darkness, One laugh
will conquer gloom.

One step must start each journey. One word
must start each prayer.
One hope will raise our spirits, One touch
can show you care.

One voice can speak with wisdom, One heart
can know what's true,
One life can make a difference, You see, it's up to you!

Blessings to Share

Today, I will tip my hat to a stranger, sharing a
kind word or smile.
Today, I will make a difference to a friend, offering
encouraging and supporting thoughts and dreams.
Today, I will be a blessing to myself, being gentle and
caring as I walk my path of life.
Today, I will be a blessing to God. He has blessed me and
I will pass that blessing on to others.
Today, I will celebrate God and scatter joy!
Life is a blessing!

Patsy and lemurs: Mutual curiosity

Anita's kitchen: A welcome refuge

Zebu cart: Modern transportation

Each one teach one

A smile is the same in every language

The Gathering Place finally finished

Everything starts with prayer

Praising God through a performance of Miraraka: A Time to Dance

All smiles after an uplifting musical performance

Blending of cultures serving in medical missions

People Reaching People friends visit a local church

The Bishop and a group of women break ground for
the Women's Center

Guest and student accommodation at the Cathedral Complex

Admiring Mesa's creations as she works in her
6 person, one room home

Created to Create

Proudly possessing sanitary napkin kits

Teaching young women how to use the Days for Girls kit

With intrigue and hope, young women learn about their
bodies through the Days for Girls program

Simple gifts bring joy

The first St. Patrick's Cathedral

The current St. Parick's Cathedral

Rev. Patsy congratulates Rev. Nolavy on her ordination day as the first female priest in the Diocese of Toliara

Rev. Patsy, Bishop Todd and Archbishop Ian Earnest, Archbishop of the Indian Ocean and Bishop of the Anglican Diocese of Mauritius

Mandraphihaona (see you later), not Veloma (goodbye)

Chapter Four

CHEMISTRY

The blessing of God the Father, who brings us together,
go on deepening our love for each other:

The blessing of God the Son, who has healed us and helped
us through battles and challenges upon our lives,
make us radiant in grace and praise:

The blessing of the Holy Spirit, who has chosen us to give
life abundantly,
go on enriching the gift we are to each other,
calling us to be a united blessing for others.

And may the blessing of God Almighty Father, Son and
Holy Spirit be with us now and forevermore.
Amen.

Patsy McGregor

Now That's Teamwork!

Excitedly a group of strong, hefty men circled up and prayed before beginning daily construction. As the workers were laying down concrete for the second floor of the new Guesthouse at St. Patrick's Cathedral Complex in 2018, Todd looked out the window proclaiming, "They are pouring concrete!"

Quickly, I got up to see what I had visualized in my head; a large concrete truck pouring concrete onto the second floor, which might take 2-3 hours to complete. But when I got to the window, third-world reality set in. TIM! (This is Madagascar!) Seventeen strong men are "pouring" concrete by handing buckets upon buckets of hand-stirred cement assembly-line style up wooden scaffolding.

Four men on the ground floor stir gravel, sand, cement and water together at the same time. After it's mixed, they shovel it into hand-made buckets and four other men pass buckets to others standing at various levels on a hand-crafted scaffolding of wood brought in by ox-cart. Buckets are lifted person-to-person to several men on the roof. These men pour, pack and level it, dropping the empty buckets back to those on the ground ready to once again shovel more hand-stirred concrete, and the assembly line continues.

Already working since early morning, they will continue this procedure through the night, guided by temporary electrical light fixtures, as this specific task must be finished within 24 hours in order for the concrete to set evenly. In Madagascar, life is about working together in community. These eager workers pass buckets, singing, shouting and encouraging one another to keep up the good work.

When Dad's pending passing was getting difficult, it was cumbersome for him to get up and use the bathroom. Exhausted from doing so, he still made great effort. Finally though, he had to succumb to depending on others to help him with this most basic human need. On one particular occasion after Mom, my sister Betsy and I helped dad to the restroom and back, his last words before falling sleep were, "Now that's teamwork!"

Teamwork. Life takes courage and we need to work together helping with challenges. Leaders with God-given calling and good character know how to work with others. Chemistry is about working as a team.

Developing relational skills does not happen by chance. Intentionally working together as a unified team, joy catches fire. Returning to joy when something goes wrong and seeing others the way God sees them creates appreciation and good chemistry with those with whom we work. Whether we are construction workers hand-pouring concrete or a daughter-mother duo helping a frail father to the bathroom, when our job is done together, we can gratefully exclaim, "Now that's teamwork!"

A Radiated Tortoise and a Lemur

As an introvert, Todd likes his tortoise days. The days when he can hibernate inside his shell, not affected by the world around him. I am more like a lemur. With a loud 'Good Morning!' cry, I open the curtains and welcome the day, swinging branch to branch with excitement. According to the Myers—Briggs Type Indicator®, our personalities fall at two extreme opposites. How is the chemistry between us? If you know us at all as a couple, you will chuckle at the question. Let's just say, sometimes, sparks fly.

Life brings challenge. We have learned, over many years, by God's grace, to be gentle to each other's weaknesses and concentrate on one another's strengths. Learning and finding the key in a relationship is so important. Sometimes the mechanisms are blocked and then the key won't budge. Some good oiling and jiggling might be necessary before picking up a hammer to knock the locked mechanism out and replace it!

Gentleness with another's weakness is not naturally my first response. One Sunday morning when there was a man, drunk, sitting in the pew, my first thoughts were of judgment. "Why is *he* here?" But since he was calm, kind and quiet, we didn't suggest that he leave and he stayed and worshipped with us. He came the next Sunday and the Sunday after that, sometimes with alcohol on his breath and other times not. Finally, he gave up alcohol all together. Now he has turned his life over to Christ and helps to lead worship on Sundays.

In the Old Testament story of Noah and his family, we read that Noah drank too much wine, became drunk and lay uncovered in his tent. Ham saw it and told his two brothers, Shem and Japheth. Shem and Japheth took a garment, laid it across their shoulders, walked in backwards and covered their father's nakedness with their faces turned the opposite way.[64] Gentle protectors, they were tender towards their father's vulnerability.

During our children's growing up years in Antananarivo, a priest gave us two lemurs as it was difficult for his family to afford to feed them anymore. The new pets seemed unique and we accepted them, calling the zoo to know if we could keep the brown fuzzy mammals as domestic pets. They gave us permission, asking us to feed and take good care of them. We called them Tic and Tac.

When it was time to clean their cages, they roamed around the front yard, tackling one another on the grass and playing with

Ali, our white Cottona dog. One day, however, Tac ambled onto the neighbor's lawn and unfortunately was killed by the neighbor's dog. Surprisingly, Ali, went over to the body and dragged it back onto our property. Innately caring for one another, God's creatures, even those of a different species, remind us of being gentle protectors.

Recently, I found a praying in color card from eleven years ago. On the back is written: "As co-workers, family members and human beings in general, may we have grace to cover people's exposure in love, causing them not to be ashamed. May we look the other way even when seeing impurities and may our love for them cover a multitude of sins. Cleanse our hearts, O God. In Jesus Name. Amen. April 29th 2009."

How do a radiated turtle and a lemur live together? By God's grace, learning to be considerate of one another, cultivating a life in common.[65]

Sequoia Trees

Sequoia trees tower hundreds of feet in the air and withstand intense environmental pressures. Fierce winds may blow and forest fires rage but the Sequoia stands firm because they interlock their roots with the sequoias around them.

Everyone needs wise counsel throughout life. A person of good character pursues it and gladly receives wisdom from others. It is essential to seek godly advice, healthy friendships and experienced mentors. Interlocking the roots of truth with another's helpful support allows us to face problems and stand strong.

The abundance of counselors brings victory. Finding a friend with whom to interlock prayer roots can make or break us when enduring the storms of life. When we intentionally live lives of grace-filled integrity, we seek others with whom to share joys and sorrows. Bishop Samitiana, the current Bishop of the Diocese of Toliara, and my husband, Todd have been friends since we first came to Madagascar. Seeking friendship and a prayer partner, my husband asked Samitiana, an unmarried priest at that time, if he would like to get together weekly and pray together. Samitiana eagerly accepted the invitation. They have remained close friends and co-workers because of this foundation of prayer.

Teamwork. Standing firm, interlocking roots with others around us. When the storms of life prevail, we will endure with an interlocking system of trusting friends sharing our joys and sorrows.

Living in Symphony

One of my favorite childhood memories was watching Arthur Fiedler conduct the Boston Pops Symphony. A myriad of instruments playing foot-tapping music together in symphony was amazing. In the Greek language, intercession means to be harmonious or symphonize. As we pray for one another it is important to be in agreement, harmonious with God and our fellow human beings. Sometimes we overlook the importance of being in harmony with ourselves.

The 15-month devotional, *The Reservoir*, starts its third week with a few major questions. "What is My Picture of Myself?"

and "Why is my picture of myself so important?" A reflection question hit the nail on the head.

> Think about a group you've been part of that struggled to work well together. Did any members of the group feel unaccepted? If so, how did that affect the team dynamics?[66]

Bingo. Acceptance. To get the twinkle back in my eye, I must get the log out of my eye. Sometimes we need to focus on the reasons why we do the things we do. In even the smallest way, do I live for or from acceptance?

As we ponder, if we truly admit it, we have been living from a foundation of seeking and achieving acceptance. If we let that soak in a little bit, we realize what a shaky foundation this is and how precarious and unreliable this can be as the storms of life come ashore.

Most likely we know God's love as an intellectual conviction. Perhaps we have even memorized verses. God is love. We know it in our heads. As a priest, I've preached it, taught it, written it, sung it. And yet, if I am truly honest, sometimes I have trouble actually feeling it. Do you too?

Meeting Desmond Tutu for the first time, I was excited. Standing in the parking lot of the cruise liner docked in Mauritius, I was hoping (and praying) to meet him and had a question ready. As God would have it, just as I arrived, he did as well. Getting out of a taxi, he came right over to me when he saw my clergy collar. Shaking hands, we greeted one another and I gave him the 300 palm fronds our congregation had folded into crosses that he had requested from the Archbishop. He wanted to bless the crosses on the cruise liner during Holy Week. During a quick snapshot I seized the opportunity.

"Archbishop Tutu, (he later asked me to call him Arch), if you had one ministry tip to give me, what would it be?" Looking directly into my eyes, his response cut to the foundation of my soul. "God loves you."

He said it slowly, distinctly, as if they were almost three separate words.

God. Loves. You.

As human beings, we have a unique place in creation. We are the only creatures made in the image of God. God's Spirit has breathed life into our very spirit. We are not our own. We are His.

Creation brings us into special relationship with God. How we treat ourselves matters. I realize (and admit) I am way too hard on myself, and others.

God calls me "very good."[67] Why do I have trouble calling myself that?

Before Jesus began his ministry, his Father publicly declared, "You are my Son, the Beloved; with you I am well pleased."[68] God publicly affirms his love for His Son. Why is it so hard for human beings to understand that we are also created "very good" and that God, our Father is also "well pleased" with us?

Living in symphony with others and being in harmony with ourselves establishes gratitude for being created, 'very good.' Spreading this gratitude to family, friends, and those with whom you work builds chemistry. Honoring another's support, the way they lend a helping hand, give advice, helping us think things through creates a team.

Life is a beautiful symphony. As we return grace to others, loving our neighbors as ourselves, we honor one another believing they are the one's God designed for us to love and learn from and to inspire, as they challenge us to be all that we are created to be.

Flipped Switch

The electricity often trips in our home. If one electrical device is being used, it trips another and our lights go out. Having lived with this for so long, sometimes I may not even realize it has been tripped. I sit in the dark, wondering when the electricity will return. In actuality, there was a mix up in installation when they were wiring the house. I go to the electrical box and flip the switch myself.

The same can be true with brains. Brains are configured to know our identity according to how others see us. We need to rewire them so they don't trip --setting our identity to what God knows about us. Friends and family cannot give us all aspects of what we need. We all have emotional birth defects, distorting our identities. Every family has missing abilities and difficulties. Instead of negativity, do we think the best of one another?

"Stop allowing yourselves to be agitated and disturbed; and do not permit yourselves to be fearful and intimidated and cowardly and unsettled."[69] I love this paraphrase of the known passage, "Peace I leave with you...not as the world gives...Do not let your hearts be troubled, neither let them be afraid."[70]

In other words, don't let your minds be tripped by the troubles of this world and agitations of others. Go to the electrical box. Flip the switch and reset your mind. It's not easy to always be a person of blessing and grace, but it is a precious part of our calling. Sometimes it's up to be the positive change we want to see.

Tolerance of another's weakness is a strong aspect of the Malagasy culture. Elders are cared for at home. Handicapped are pushed on handcrafted apparatus replacing wheelchairs. When I fell at the Gathering Place and tore my knee ligaments in two places, it took months to find crutches. Unable to do things myself, I was mobilized by the community. Grace upon grace.

The same applies in a spiritual sense. Growing strong requires seeking the Lord through his word as well as spending time with an older and stronger Christian through discipleship. We need one another.

Perhaps many people in the world are blessed not to have a morning paper on their doorstep, or internet 24/7. Perhaps it gives them more time to ponder the beauty of God's creation. Spending days outside, cooking, washing clothes and chatting with a friend or family member under the shade tree releases joy and peace.

Thanking the people with whom we work makes them feel seen and celebrated. Treating one another with grace helps us believe the best of each other, What if we woke up this morning with only what we thanked God for yesterday? Would there be anybody else living in your house? Sometimes I wonder if my husband would be sleeping next to me.

With a mind occupied with thanking God, there are fewer occasions for the electrical switch flipping our brains to worry or complain. Negative thought patterns gradually grow weaker and weaker and the lights stay connected, all night long.

Raising Warriors

Strong hands rested upon me as a thumb pressed holy oil, forming a cross on my forehead symbolizing God's anointing. Archbishop Benjamin Nzimbi blessed my ordination as a priest on September 3, 2005, at All Saints Church, Nairobi in the Anglican Diocese of Kenya.

On the same day, in another country's capital across the Mozambique Channel of the Indian Ocean, a small child, not yet a year old, is wrapped in a cloth and carried on her mother's breast as her mother does her daily marketing. Reaching out her tiny hand to passers-by, she places it on their heads and spontaneously proclaims "Amen."

Fourteen years later, during the Coronavirus outbreak, with school cancelled for months, this same child, now a young lady, spent mornings with me as we played guitars passed on by friends. We talked. We wondered. What will another 14 years bring? She will be twenty-eight. I will be seventy-five. Will we both still be singing and playing guitar? Will we still be intentionally listening and following, walking our God-ordained paths? Raised as warriors, are we ready for life ahead?

It is important to remember that God has fully equipped us to handle whatever comes our way. What we need is help to use the God-given equipment. The Word of God is our sword.

Dealing with some inner wobblies of life, I went to a prayer counselor trained in inner healing. During a peaceful and life-giving session, she emphatically declared, "*You carry a very large sword. Do you know where your sword is?*" Wide-eyed and very surprised, I bluntly replied, "*No.*" Spiritually speaking, she pointed it out. "*There it is. It's right on your back.*"

The Holy Spirit leads, guides and intercedes. Jesus paid the full sacrifice on Calvary. The Trinity is complete and fully able to equip us with everything we need. Are you ready to be a warrior? Do you know where your sword is?

Raising warriors is something we concentrate on when building disciples. Asking God to raise up an army, we looked for durability. God is not careless. When difficulties come into our lives, especially events we think God could have prevented, we may feel God is careless, being unfair. But God promises to be our constant companion, caring for us, protecting us every step of our journey. It is important to remember we are being raised as a warrior, not as a sofa-sitting Christian. Designed to be in the battle, it's important to be spiritually fit, confident, equipped for the fight with God at the helm.

Having this attitude is critical to our mind-set. When trials enter our lives, we will be armed, not alarmed. Until we reach our ultimate home in heaven, we will be at war.

Pope Francis reminds us, "The Bible says that the life of Christians is a military undertaking that requires fighting against evil"[71] Sarah Young counsels, "Adopting a wartime mentality makes it easier to handle difficulties as they arise. Don't waste time and energy bemoaning your circumstances, avoid the trap of feeling singled out for hardship."[72] And, to be prepared in this battle, the Rev. Dr. Francis MacNutt, a tower in the healing ministry, wrote prayers of protection and cleansing from evil used by many in the healing ministry. [73] Faith and tenacity undergird us as we experience suffering from evil.

Life includes spiritual battles, sickness, trials and tribulations – way more than our humanity can bear. We need God's healing, refilling, life-giving vibrancy to replenish us. Daily, we enforce the will of God here on earth by praying His Word. If this is neglected, it is like letting a gang of robbers take over a good neighborhood. Without the regular presence of spiritual police (i.e., God's hosts of angels) to maintain peace and order, thugs are free to roam. We have a battle to fight - for our own lives and also for the sake of others. We are God's generals – called to enforce, with His authority, what He wants done on this earth!

Are you brave enough to be a warrior? This is God's will for us, building competency. We are admonished to stand firm and to be brave. By his mighty power at work within us, He is able to accomplish infinitely more than we would ever dare to ask or hope.[74] As God spoke to Isaiah, he speaks to us today. "Fear not, for I am with you: Be not dismayed, for I am your God. I will strengthen you. Yes, I will help you. I will uphold you with my righteous right hand."[75]

Responding to the Call

"Victor," I asked one day. "You are from Kenya. Why did you decide to be a missionary in Madagascar?"

Victor replies. *"When Bishop Todd came to recruit people to join you both in Madagascar, he said there was a great need. At that time, I was working at Holy Trinity, Anglican Church of Kenya. There were more staff and clergy at that one church than Bishop Todd would be working with in the whole Diocese of Toliara, an area a fourth the size of Kenya. God had already impressed in my heart a desire to be a blessing to other nations. I realized this was my call. The harvest is plentiful and workers are few. I responded to this call, did my own fundraising, and followed the Lord who was sending me into the harvest."* (May 2008 Victor came to Madagascar in partnership with the Anglican Church of Kenya and Church Army.)

Before people hear the gospel in the south, the majority of people make sacrifices to their ancestors. Goats and chickens are often sacrificed. Living among taboos and superstitions, people worry about what they are doing. For example, they may warn another, "Don't turn left when going to the market." Sharing the gospel is a joy. When they accept Christ, there is no turning back. They have given up everything. With great faith and courage, they trust and turn their life around.

When Victor came to Madagascar in 2008, he did not think he would be staying for long. At the time of writing, it has been over 12 years. We all need a safe place to share, care, pray, grow and serve. When people feel safe, they are inclined to stay. Life was never intended for us to be alone. Thanks be to God! We live it together. And guess what? Victor met Nolavy, our former neighbor and the first female priest ordained in Diocese of Toliara. They got married, now have two children and are expecting a third, and are a strong clergy couple with determination to honor one another and glorify God in worship, faithfulness and obedience.

Feelings of worth flourish in an atmosphere of love. Transformational words of blessing greatly impact one another and the community. When differences are appreciated, mistakes tolerated and communication is open, we are blessed to be a blessing. With God, we never know what lovely surprises life might bring!

Splendid Torch

Nights can be dark, very dark. In many parts of the world only a few candles light up many communities. When a candle is lit, a path is lit for others.

The image of letting our light shine is a powerful one. Created by God to shine, we are to hold our candles high, giving light to our surroundings. As George Bernard Shaw once wrote, "Life is no brief candle. It is a splendid torch which I hold for the moment, and I want to make it burn as brightly as possible before handing it on to future generations."[76]

Is life for you, a 'splendid torch?' With light, our hearts grow bigger, round like a full moon, soft like the whispers of wildlife. Life giving and life affirming, our spirits enter into peace. Life as a splendid torch brings warmth and kindness into the depths of our souls and illuminates our surrounding communities.

Years ago, when we were in seminary, Todd and I had the honor of having a private 15-minute conversation with J. I. Packer, one of the most influential evangelical leaders of our time. We had a specific question to ask him. The reputation of the Episcopal Church was especially going through hardship and we asked, *"How do you remain within the church even among such disputes?"*

Profoundly, J. I. Packer replied. *"I have learned to be content within my discontent."*

Considering J. I. Packer's wisdom causes me to wonder if I am comfortable within discomfort. If I am not comfortable with discomfort, then how can I be a strategist for change? Life is flowing, like roaring rapids, not a stagnant pool. Am I willing to sit in discomfort, without trying to solve the problem, and listen while another works out their difficulty? We must have hard conversations even when we're not ready.

Though we may sit in darkness, God is always our light. Sometimes even in the light, we are meant to rest in the shadows. Knowing when to rest enhances our work place. If we continue pushing ourselves, ignoring how worn out we are, we may collapse altogether. While resting in the shadows, God refreshes our spirit, mind and body. Fully present with us at all times, God shelters us in the shadowy place, nurturing us under his wings, covering us with his feathers. Under his wings we find refuge, his faithfulness is our shield and rampart.[77]

Complaints snuff out our candle. As we hold our lights for one another, forgetting the power of blessing in the work place and the joy we experience working together, can quench our God-given candles. Words of affirmation and gratitude relight the flame.

The deepest ache of the soul is the spiritual longing for connection and belonging. No one was created for isolation.[78] The light of Christ shines from within. Shining his brightest smile on our hearts, God's love is revealed in never ending ways. Knowing Christ and making him known is a blessing to all. Working together, life can be a splendid torch!

Light the Fire

Like a solitary piece of charcoal, if one's spirituality is left to itself, it gets cold and dies out. But living in Christian community strengthens one another. With many pieces of coal in the fire, the embers keep burning. There is less chance of the fire dying. In Madagascar people first light their cooking fire by going to another person to take a piece of their burning coal. This is a metaphor for Christianity and the process of evangelism and discipleship. Once our own spiritual fire is lit, we have a calling to share the charcoal with others. It's time to help others light their fire, live transparent lives of close proximity to one another and keep each other accountable in the faith.

Living into what we want in life and what God is calling us to do requires intention. 1 Peter 3:15 urges us to always be ready to "give a reason for the hope that is within you." Reaching out to others in an approachable and reasonable manner with love and respect will go beyond theological jargon and will allow the gospel to be passed on to others. By living an example of faith, we persuade people that Christianity makes sense. This tilling of the ground allows faith seeds to flourish. Some prepare the soil, some plant, some water, but it's God who causes the growth. By living transparent and authentic lives, we prepare for an upcoming harvest.

Ultimately a person's spiritual life is up to them; we are there to assist. Relational evangelism allows dialogue, helping people find faith through friendship and bringing them into Christian community. 2 Timothy 2:2 is a constant reminder of our calling to mentor and teach one another. "Teach these great truths to trustworthy people who are able to pass them on to others." When people live in community, there is an opportunity to naturally share faith and disciple one another.

This relational approach to evangelism engages people in conversation, allowing people to reach out and understand others, building trust and a healthy environment for sharing the gospel. Survival of the church and our own spiritual lives depends upon outreach and discipleship.

It only takes a spark to get a fire going. Perhaps it is one person lighting a match and another taking a piece of coal from another's cooking fire. The whole purpose of our calling is to help one another get refined through the fire, purified by the grace of God and become all God has intended.

Opportunities for Personal Reflection

Meditate on the words of Pope Francis below. How can you light up your world?

In our times, as we are all aware, some people's lives can end up mediocre and dull because they probably do not go in search of real treasure: they are content with attractive but fleeting things, whose bright lights prove illusory as they give way to darkness. Instead, the light of the Kingdom is not like fireworks, it is light: fireworks last only an instant, whereas the light of the Kingdom accompanies all our life.[79]

Lord, thank you for your truth that sets all people free. Give me wisdom, patience and courage as I work with others, speaking only what you call me to speak and listening only to what you speak to me. May my words, as a sacred tool, pierce through the darkness, a sword bringing forth truth and manifesting God's love. Used for your glory and the building of the body of Christ, please consecrate my speech this day. In Jesus name I pray, Amen.

Chapter Five

COMPETENCY

Live as if you were to die tomorrow.
Learn as if you were to live forever.
Mahatma Ghandi

Knock-Knock

Have you played the childhood game, Knock-Knock? From time to time, I play one with God.

Me: "*Knock, Knock.*"

God: "*Who's there?*" (With a child's game we don't argue over theology and the fact that God already knows who is asking....)

Me: "*Me!*"

God: "*Me, Who?*"

Me: "*Knock, Knock.*"

God: "*Who's there?*"

Me: "*Me!*"

God: "*Me, Who?*"

Me: "*Knock, Knock.*"

God: "*Who's there?*"

Me: "*Me...again...*"

God: "*Me, again, who?*"

Me: "*Me, again...and I won't stop until you answer my prayer!*"

Have you ever had to wait on God to answer your prayer? Life brings us on journeys and detours and sometimes a dead end. Sometimes we need to keep on knocking, like Gaston. "*Bishop Todd, I want to become a priest.*" "*I am sorry, Gaston, You must have a High School Diploma to apply for theological school,*" Bishop Todd replied.

Determined, Gaston promised he would study hard. He asked for help to pay school fees in order to take an intensive course to help him to study for a High School Diploma/BACC. Graciously, Todd accepted his request. Unfortunately, Gaston did not pass.

"*Knock, Knock.*" Gaston asked again. He wanted to take the exam a second time. Would we help pay school fees? Generously, my husband agreed. Unfortunately, Gaston did not pass.

"*Knock, Knock.*" Still longing to get his BACC, Gaston asked a third time. Would we help pay school fees again?

"*I am sorry, Gaston. You will now have to find your own funds to study for your high school/BACC degree,*" responded my husband. And Gaston found the funds, took the exam a third time, and did not pass. Undaunted, Gaston took the exam again the next year and did not pass for a fourth time. Persistent and determined, Gaston gave it one more try.

Knock, Knock. God, do you hear me? I want to serve you, as a priest. In order to do so, I need to pass this exam. Will you please help me?!

The fifth attempt in taking the exam, Gaston passed. Jumping up and down when he heard the results, he grinned ear to ear. A year later he was gifted a scholarship to attend three years of seminary in the capital of Madagascar, Antananarivo. Gaston is now a deacon and has been accepted for ordination as a priest.

Sometimes competency is not how much we know or how talented we are, but how we persevere in order to get to where we are going. Pray that you'll have the strength to stick it out over the long haul – not the grim strength of gritting your teeth but the glory-strength God gives. It is strength that endures the unendurable and spills over into joy.[80] As Albert Einstein once observed, "Wisdom is not a product of schooling but of the life-long attempt to acquire it."

No one can go back and start a new beginning, but anyone can start today and make a new ending. Just ask Gaston.

"Do You Have a Pen?"

Walking through hot sand on her way to school, a young girl stopped me on the dirt path. Looking into my eyes, she pleaded in Malagasy, *"Do you have a pen?"*

"Azafady," I responded, not in the habit of carrying a pen on my morning walk. I was sorry I could not deliver on her request. Her humble appeal could change her future and as I continued my walk, I silently prayed the Lord would help her find a pen. Sometimes competency can only be shown after receiving the simple tools needed to move forward in education.

Equipping others makes me consider. Am I a strength finder[81] in other people's lives? Do I help provide others with the tools they need to move forward in life? It might even be as simple as a word of encouragement, a silent prayer or a ball-point pen.

Opportunities arose for many by teaching young women how to hold scissors and cut airplane magazines into strips of paper. Rolling paper around a simple toothpick, they would glue it; varnish it; and, make the paper into a bead. Tantelly was one girl who thrived with her new talents.

Although gifted intellectually, Tantelly stopped going to school her final year of secondary school to get married and have a baby. In order to earn income for her family, she began to make cards and paper beads with Lucia in my small open-air office.

As Tantelly created beads, she also began to realize that God created her. As God's workmanship, we are created in Christ Jesus for good works. He invites each of us to join with Jesus in the work he has prepared for us to do.[82] God prepared this road before hand that we should walk in it.

After two years of growing in her talents and creativity, Tantelly desired to finish her secondary school education. Her dream was to study and become a mid-wife.

A friend gave me money to offer her a partial study scholarship. Added to the earnings received by her own income from making handicrafts, Tantelly was able to study and pass her BACC with honors. She continued her education and enrolled in a mid-wife program. Working hard through her studies, her dream has come true. Tantelly recently completed the mid-wife curriculum and has become a mid-wife.

Knowing Christ lives in us can exponentially change our lives, if we let it. Leaning on, trusting in and competent in Christ alone, God's compassion is overflowing. Reliance is in God, not on others nor our own insight or understanding.[83] Joyfully, God makes his abode in our humble, human-body homes and works on renovating us from the inside out. Knowing this fills our hearts with joy and when we invite him in, God comes to stay

Stepping Out

When a few bold women stepped into the space of following their passion and developing their God-given gifts, more women followed. My already small office needed expansion. Money was raised and a Women's Center was built for women to continue to make handicrafts and Days for Girls sanitary napkin kits. This was an answer for girls and women who often used banana peels to absorb their menstruation. And protect their clothes and dignity.

Discipling young women in Madagascar, I was encouraged by their perseverance. I learned from them and gave back to them love and honor. A November 2019 article in The National Geographic observed, "If we want to push our daughters to compete side by side with our sons, we have to be willing to teach them to be comfortable with making someone else uncomfortable with their talent and success."[84] Perhaps I was a role model to them. As the only white woman priest in a country the size of Texas, and in an Anglican province that covered the Indian Ocean, I was stepping out in faith believing in the women who would follow. At times, it would be excruciatingly difficult. Often, I felt drained and unappreciated. As Eleanor Roosevelt reflected, "A woman is like a tea bag. No one really knows her strength until steeped in hot water." I guess God saw the strength in me, even when I did not see it in myself.

In Madagascar, as in other parts of the world, the message of empowerment has not been reinforced for girls and women. Many times, we have to go against the flow of culture and the voices in our own heads. Women who want to change the world, or go as far as their talents and interests take them, sometimes have to resist or reject that little voice in their heads that stokes our insecurities and suggests how we should or shouldn't behave.[85]

Let's remember the words of Pope Francis:

> In the history of salvation, it was a woman who welcomed God's Word. Women too kept alive the flame of faith in the dark night, awaiting and then proclaiming the Resurrection. Women find deep and joyful fulfilment in precisely these two acts: welcoming and proclaiming. They are the protagonists of a Church that goes forth, listening and caring for the needs of others, capable of fostering true processes of justice and bringing the warmth of a home to the various social environments where they find themselves. Listening, reflection and loving activity: these are the elements of a joy ever renewed and shared with others through feminine insight, the care of creation, the gestation of a more just world, and the creation of a dialogue that respects and values differences.[86]

Teach What You Know

Believing a young girl had musical ability, I handed her a broken guitar. Glued together at the neck, it was the best I had to offer. As a starter guitar for a youthful Malagasy girl, it was a gift. When I gave her the guitar, she was excited and inquisitive at the same time. *"How am I going to learn? Will you teach me?"*

"I have never taught guitar before..." I mumbled reluctantly, *"...and I only know a handful of chords. But, I will teach you what I know."*

Already having studied violin, she had a musical foundation. It wasn't long until she surpassed my knowledge of chords. Softly, she questioned me one day. *"Neny, isn't this the fingering for the E chord?"* I had been getting E, Em and E7 mixed up from time to time. By her diligently practicing and learning the sheet of guitar chords, this young musician gently guided me to increase my capacity to play the chords the correct way.

One of our keys to leadership in founding the Diocese of Toliara, was to bring another alongside with you, training one another as you go. As we teach discipleship, we emphasize, "Just teach what you know."

Not being an expert on a topic can be intimidating. However, move forward any way, even when feeling inadequate for the task. For many years I declined when people asked me to teach them guitar. Never having been formally taught and only knowing a few simple chords, I didn't think I was good enough. Then one day it dawned on me. If I don't teach this person, they might not ever have another chance. So, in spite of how basic my knowledge, I teach what I know.

Understanding ourselves is necessary for competency. Instead of focusing on our inadequacy, imperfection or even doubt and worry, make every effort to stay connected with the Father.

Our deep inadequacy is wrapped in God's boundless sufficiency. We don't have to have it all together. Actually, that is an illusion. It's important that we know our strengths and weaknesses, but most important of all, stay focused on the Father.

When choosing disciples, find a person strong in the 3 T's: Time, Trust and Teachability. Building relationships takes time. Do they have enough time to be a disciple? Do they trust you? Are they teachable? Spending time with the person will help you decide if they are up to the challenge of being a role model to others.

One Easter Monday, on a church picnic at the beach, I found a young woman with these attributes. Dipping my toes into the Indian Ocean, several women came to join me. Slowly I ventured deeper into the water; ankles, calf, and just above the knee. Some turned back. But a few stood by my side. One grabbed my hand, curiously desiring to go deeper.

"*Te hianatra ve ianao?*" "Would you like to learn?" I asked in Malagasy.

Some nodded, other's shook their head. One looked directly into my eyes. "*Eny. Te hianatra aho.*" "*Yes, I want to learn.*"

Coaxing her to trust me, she learned to float. Her interest was palpable. I found her teachable. As it turned out, she was my next-door neighbor. How convenient for spending time together! That made up the 3 T's! Time. Trust. Teachable.

We didn't know it at the time, but the woman who learned how to float has become the first woman priest in the Diocese of

Toliara. This gives us hope for others. Maybe the 14-year-old girl with a broken guitar will someday become a worship leader herself. Developing competency begins with spending time with those we trust and being teachable to learn new things. We never know where the opportunity might lead.

Hydrated?

A stateside masseuse, trusted friend and devout Christian once told me, "You need to drink more water. Your skin is hydrated, but your muscles are not."

Shocked, I hadn't realized that I needed to drink water for my muscles. Brenda explained, "Hydration needs to go down deep, past the surface, into the deepest parts of the body." The metaphor applies spiritually. Drinking living water for the soul saturates God's love into the most intimate parts of our inner beings.

Orchestrating infrastructure and creating a diocese has taken extreme effort. Initiating programs and fundraising millions of dollars over the years has taken perseverance and drive. Feeding the poor, distributing cyclone relief, building churches, schools, an Educational Center, the Women's Center, health clinics and two Cathedrals has been exhilarating and extremely exhausting at the same time.

What has kept us going? Drinking hundreds of thousands of gallons of God's living water, spiritual disciplines and prayer. It takes a deep personal reservoir to keep spiritually hydrated in the spiny desert of southern Madagascar.

Simply put, spiritual disciplines are practices of friendship with God. The purpose of spiritual practice is to do just that – practice! Transformation of mind, body, soul and spirit takes dedication and commitment. The Diocese of Toliara focuses on six disciplines: Daily devotions, Discipleship, Evangelism, Giving, Fasting and Obedience to God and the Scriptures.

Spiritual disciplines are not always hard, although they can be quite demanding. The primary requirement is to hydrate our longing and thirst for God. Friendship with God is not a series of religious duties but rather a relationship. Jesus himself said, "I do not call you servants any longer...but I have called you friends."[87]

Paul's analogy of a farmer and his field is useful. A farmer is helpless to grow grain; all he can do is plant the seeds in the right conditions for growing grain. This is the way with spiritual disciplines – they are a way of sowing the Spirit. The disciplines are God's way of setting the environment and getting us rooted into the ground; putting us in a sacred space where God can work within us and transform us.

By themselves, the spiritual disciplines can do nothing. They are God's means of grace. We place ourselves where God can bless us and enter into a conscious choice of action. The path does not produce the change. It only places us in the environment where the change can occur. To the extent that we enter the path, God's gracious work will take over our inner spirit, transforming ingrained habits.

Walking on the path of disciplined grace for a season, we are blessed with new treasures. Surprisingly, in unguarded moments we discover internal changes. Spontaneous flow of the Spirit bubbles from our inner sanctuary, manifesting fruits: Love, joy, peace, patience, kindness, generosity, faithfulness, gentleness and self-control come more readily to our fingertips and tongues.[88]

Growing into a familiar relationship with God, creates an emotional and spiritual space, allowing Christ to construct an inner sanctuary in our heart. Meditation and prayer send us into our ordinary world with perspective and balance. Having a spiritual thirst is healthy. Keeping spiritually hydrated is imperative.

What does it take to be a competent leader? Suppose we are not changed so much by what we know but by whom we love? Perhaps the number one priority for competent leadership is love, only love.

My husband says, *"The church is to be a place where we are changed."*[89] Let's be a part of that change, by hydrating ourselves spiritually and cultivating the soil for God to work within us as we lean on, trust in, and are confident in the Lord with all our hearts and minds.[90]

Come Alive!

"Hey girls! Do you want to go into the rainforest with me and journey in a dugout canoe?"my husband Todd asked our daughters Corbi and Charese.

Answering quickly, the girls came running. *"Yes! Let's go, Dad!"*

A few years prior to this enticement, Todd walked over 100 miles into the rainforest to spread the gospel message. When a town drunk heard the gospel message, he received God's love with open arms, dedicated his life to the Lord and burned all his witchcraft paraphernalia. Soon after that, he became an evangelist, under Todd's tutelage.

When we left Madagascar to move to Kenya, this man, Donné, had been totally transformed and his faith was on fire. Bishop Remi was impressed by his incredible exuberance to share the gospel and his competence in planting many churches. Donné was sent to the unreached areas of the region of Toliara.

When Todd was elected Bishop of the Toliara missionary area, Donné was already planting churches in southern Madagascar. When we moved back to Madagascar, Evangelist Donné and his family were thrilled to greet us. He now had local support and a leader by his side.

Over and over again, Evangelist Donné asked Todd to ordain him as a priest. Much like the persistence of Gaston in the *knock-knock* story shared previously, Todd was reluctant to ordain Donne because he did not meet the church's educational standards. Due to the lack of available schools in the rainforest, Donné only had a 4th grade education.

Very much a servant of the Lord, Donné continued to be an evangelist and planted several more churches. People saw the Holy Spirit at work. Todd recommended his ordination to Bishop Remi and the bishop approved it. What has been the result of one man, with a fourth-grade education, who is on fire for the Lord? Thousands of people have come to faith, several churches have been planted and a number of emerging leaders from the south of Madagascar came alive. This is a model of true competency.

Competency is the ability to do something successfully or efficiently. According to vocabulary.com,[91] *competency* means "capability." Although we use it to mean someone who has demonstrated qualifications, it comes from the word *compete*, meaning that someone with competency is good enough to compete with other candidates.

When Desmond Tutu was a boy, he was hospitalized for 20-months with tuberculosis. Father Trevor Huddleston, a priest in Sophiatown and a leader in the anti-apartheid movement, faithfully visited him, bringing him books to read. This had a profound impact. In retrospect, Tutu explains, "You never know! Who are the people we think we are emulating, and who the people are who have really impressed us?"[92]

Competency requires action.

> Some of the most eloquent witnesses to the Christian gospel are those who are side by side with people in need, incarnating God's concern and love. If they do that with integrity people may ask, "What makes you want to do this?" And then you have the opportunity to say, "I am here really because I love Jesus, and Jesus has impelled me to come here and I hope that my touch will be to some extent his touch."[93]

"Go...and do whatever it is that makes you come alive! Ask yourself what makes you come alive, and go do that, because what the world needs is people who have come alive."[94]

Toliara

As a port city, Toliara, Madagascar literally means *Toly eroa*: *"mooring down there."*[95] Located approximately 300 miles off the mainland of Africa it was established for trade and commerce. The earliest Europeans were a group of 600 shipwrecked Portuguese sailors in 1527. During the 16th and 17th centuries, it became a favored destination for the spice traders and at one point, the British attempted to establish a colony.

However, it was not a success. The original 140 settlers whittled down to 60 through disease and murder. The colonists left in 1646 and fifty years later St. Augustine Bay was a haven for pirates. Replicas of slave bracelets are still sold at the local market. The culture invited hospitality, but murder, slavery and selfish greed usurped good intentions.

When the university was built in 1971, Toliara became a center for education, and people came to live with friends and relatives so they could study. However, the surrounding moral environment was particularly degenerate due to the already existing sex trade. People offering their own bodies, or another's, for commerce and income is not uncommon; and, it is not helped by foreigners who travel to Madagascar for sex tourism and to participate in the trafficking of women and children.

Interestingly enough, now back in the USA, I live in an area previously known for pirates. The water was so shallow many ships would ground and pirates would steal the treasures of gold and other valuables or they would be lost at sea. Our struggle is not only against poverty, filth and political corruption. In Toliara, I could actually feel the spiritual oppression. Here on the Treasure Coast, one can be swayed by material possessions. Large mansions dot the Intracoastal and Ocean persuading the average American that they need the same.

Ephesians 6:10-11 gives us a command to "Be strong in the Lord and in the strength of his might." This is not optional for Christians. The truth of the matter is that Christians are engaged in an invisible war and in order to fight, we need to be properly dressed and put on the full armor of God.[96]

The lifestyle of putting on the armor implies a consistent and constant effort. Just as we would clothe ourselves to protect our bodies from weather, we clothe ourselves spiritually to protect us from the world, the flesh and the devil. Remember: We do not fight *for* victory, we fight *from* victory, for Jesus Christ has already defeated Satan.[97]

Bring It On!

Frightened, I was rattled. With a huge funnel cloud coming right at us, there was nowhere to run. The wise woman in the dream said, "*We just have to hunker down and ride out the storm.*"

Rolling out of bed, I was relieved it was only a dream. And yet, I have had storm dreams before and a few times they have come before life threatening situations. I dreaded another high stress problem. Was the Lord preparing me for an upcoming event? If so, I needed to be ready. I pondered the dream and decided the important thing was not the storm itself but rather my reaction to the storm.

The world-wide COVID-19 pandemic had grounded all international flights and our planned date to leave Madagascar was nearing, I thought maybe I was worried about not being able to fly back to America in time for Christmas. Wanting to spend the holidays with family, I had to mentally prepare for a disappointment. I prayed, deeply.

A few days after this dream I was laying on my bed, praying. Coming to my mind was the dream. And then, there was Jesus right before the storm. Hmmm. I wondered what would be Jesus' reaction to the huge funnel cloud bearing down. Jesus raised both arms in victory and shouted, "Bring it on!"

Confidence. Unwavering assurance. Trust. Conviction. In all circumstances. Cyclone, hurricane, forest fire or tsunami, Jesus deals with it all.

We Are Together

Soap, shampoo, body lotion, deodorant, nail polish-- all basic items that a woman from the western world takes for granted. But for most Malagasy woman, these items are out of reach. In Toliara, I saw the prevalence of sex trafficking and sex tourism. As a woman and an ordained priest, it broke my heart when I did my grocery shopping and saw a young Malagasy girl with an older European man who temptingly encouraged her, saying, "*Buy anything you want, dear*." In addition to receiving these luxury beauty products, she would be taken to a resort hotel on the beach.

She would have indoor plumbing. Her bed would be made for her. She would be served at a dinner table with silverware; and, she would be the center of attention for a week or two. If she performed well, perhaps this lifestyle could be extended another few weeks or longer. And maybe, just maybe, the man she was with would fall in love with her, take her away from poverty and fly her to another country. Just like in the movie *Pretty Woman*, her life would be changed forevermore.

Seeing a young woman believe in the possibility of this false hope made me want to scream. Even more, it made me want to take the young woman's hand and walk her right out of the store, leaving that man behind. But really, what could I do? I felt like my hands were tied. Lifting the women and their situations up to the Lord, I asked God to do something. When I felt unable to do anything, I prayed.

In retrospect, the heartbreak for the impoverished Malagasy woman who had to sell her own self in order to feed her family became the impetus for my ministry. It fueled my drive for women's ordination because women need women. It later became the theme of a musical called *Miaraka: A Time to Dance* that I wrote with my friend Collette Maurel, a fellow guitar player and writer whom I had met on the beach in Mauritius.

Miaraka is the Malagasy word for together. The story of *Miaraka: A Time to Dance* was born through darkness, heartache, a light of hope and that need to awaken worldwide consciousness to global issues such as poverty, human trafficking and prostitution. A modern-day version of the story of Mary of Magdalena. Mary is a prostitute who finds herself drowned in dark thoughts of suicide. Left on her own and without any hope of a better future, God intervenes in her life. Through the kindness of a new friend, Mary is able to taste and see real true love, the love of God. But this is not the end, she is now able to live her newborn faith among others and share what she experienced. Life with God is a celebration! Scattering joy to all she meets, life is lived together, in community. Life is now *A Time to Dance!*

Women in ministry offer a gentle touch and warmth to the church. When women know that the church encourages and supports them to be in a position traditionally held only by men, they are honored. Their talents and contributions are valued and welcomed. This is validation for women who feel called by God to serve as lay leaders and priests and offers them an opportunity to develop as well-rounded servant leaders for Christ. The equal participation of women in all positions of faith offers the community with a previously unacknowledged voice and a more inclusive perspective.

Torchbearer

While the ordination of women was approved in 2006 at the Provincial level, the ordination of women in the Dioceses of the Malagasy Episcopal Church was generally not embraced. Out of respect for the position of the Malagasy church, I put my collar on the shelf.

After being ordained six years and living in Toliara for five, I was asked by the Archbishop of the Province of the Indian

Ocean, who was also the Bishop of Mauritius, to help serve the church in Mauritius. Archbishop Ian Ernest wanted to initiate women's ordination into his Diocese and needed a seasoned, ordained woman to pioneer this endeavor. He wanted to be a history maker and asked me to join that process. Being a torchbearer in Mauritius enticed me.

When agreeing to an interview in the Mauritian paper a few months after my arrival, I was asked why women's ordination is so important. My response was this.

> "Appointing women as leaders of the church is not about doing a man's job in a man's way. It is about offering our priceless qualities and gifts to bring wholeness to the church. Strengths indwelt in women include tenderness, compassion, understanding of and nurturing others. Women have a gift of relating to and interacting with others. This interaction is needed in the church. Women offer beauty in the garden of life."[98]

Leaders are responsible to make sure that all believers are equipped for ministry. God's will for every believer is spiritual maturity and God calls all believers to minister to the world and the church. Service in the body of Christ isn't limited to one's gender. In God's army, we've been drafted into service. Every Christian is created for ministry. It is part of our identity in Christ.

Gifted leaders are not to do all the work, but to train others to carry on the work of ministry. In Madagascar we count on others to help with chores of daily life. Laundry is washed by hand and after returning from the market, vegetables need to be soaked in bleach to kill any lingering parasites. Just as I have trained our housekeeper, Jeanette, to make banana bread, brochettes and pizza, we train lay leaders of the church to help with discipleship and evangelism. Discipleship is not a program for ministry, but a life-long commitment and lifestyle.

Potential church leaders come to the Cathedral Complex from all parts of Madagascar to live in community and be trained in evangelism and church leadership at St. Patrick's Bible College. We have constant interaction with these students. Just by walking outside our door, we come in contact with the community. Students congregate in front of their living quarters, singing, playing the guitar, or just chatting in the shade.

Lifestyle evangelism and discipleship enable spiritual reproduction and train others to carry on the work of ministry. Not only are we torchbearers, we are torch-lighters. Sometimes this means extending beyond traditional boundaries to model a Christ-like lifestyle while committing to the Great Commandment and the Great Commission. Both men and woman are called to be torchbearers and live out their call from God. As Ephesians 4:1 challenges us, "Live out your calling, for you have been called by God." When God calls us to a mission, that mission is open to all.

September 23rd, 2012 had to be one of the most joyous days of my life. A few years before, Todd and I talked about the top 10 days of our lives, reminiscing our wedding day 26 years earlier, the birth of both of our daughters, meeting Queen Elizabeth twice at Buckingham Palace, our days of ordination as priests, Todd's consecration day as Bishop, our daughter's graduation from college and Corbi and Joe's wedding day. Also, I would have to add September 23rd, 2012 to the list of favorites.

My name was penned on history's pages as the first woman priest inducted into a parish to serve in the Anglican Diocese of Mauritius. When planning for this day with the Archbishop and Churchwardens of St. Simon's the Fisherman, we decided that we would prefer a local, low-key function, mostly because of such details as there was no church building yet and we were meeting in the Roman Catholic Church Hall which served as a library during the week. However, instead of a quiet and unpretentious gathering, the media got wind of what was happening. The day before, not only was there a full two-page article interviewing me, the Anglican Archbishop and the Roman Catholic Vicar General, but the Mauritian Broadcasting Corporation came on that glorious Sunday. Surprisingly, I felt quite confident that they captured me playing guitar and singing "We have come to worship You, Lord." I even played it twice again later that evening on national television.

I remember the moments of procession, climbing the steps outside the church hall/library building where we had somehow managed to remove all the tables and extra books in order to squeeze 114 chairs in a room where we normally had seated fifty. The children, waiting outside to perform their offertory youth dance gave me a thumbs up. They had loved me from the beginning.

Torch Lighters

Whether male or female the role of a priest is to be torch lighters and take care of parishioners who have been entrusted to our care. This means feeding parishioners the Word, taking care of them like a mother may take care of her children. The main task is to be a torch lighter and support others in their spiritual journey. This is done in a variety of ways such as presiding at the Eucharist, preaching, teaching, listening to confession, leading prayer groups, caring for youth and families. And in all of this, our role is to come alongside, encourage, light a torch and be a friend to others. Since at least half of the church parishioners are women, it only makes sense to have women as liturgical leaders in the church.

A feminine sensitivity and perspective is an asset in the Church and the presence of men and women as clergy working together, offers fullness to the church. Just as in many cultures women hesitate to go to a male medical doctor, having women as priests creates a more open invitation to the whole community.

In our advisory role as priests, there are often situations when it is best for a woman to listen to a female parishioner seeking advice. For example, when a woman is crying, I can comfort her, put my hand on hers and even embrace her. But if a man does this gesture, this can lead to all sorts of interpretations and possible misunderstandings that may affect his validation as a priest. Often women may feel more comfortable talking to another woman. This understanding can ignite a woman's spiritual life.

Imagine a Christmas Eve candlelight service. One person starts as the torchbearer; she holds her lit candle steady and upright. The next person comes and lights his candle. Then, holding his candle steady and upright he turns to his neighbor who now lights her candle and holds it steady and upright.

This is repeated until the candle of every person in the community is lit. Each person now becomes a torchbearer and holds a candle steady and upright for others to come and be a torch lighter.

Opportunities for Personal Reflection

Has God ever knocked at your heart?
How did you respond?

Competency

What are the gifts and talents God has given you?
Are you developing them?
Are you using them?
Are you sharing them?
Are you teaching what you know?

Perseverance

Is God calling you?
How do you prepare to answer the Call?
Do you need to prepare or just DO?

When have you been a torch lighter?
When have you been a torch bearer?

Chapter Six

COMMUNITY

From my face, is the smile of welcome.
From my arms is the embrace of love.
May others feel loved and blessed.
Let me run to them even before they know
I am coming their way.
Patsy McGregor

Kely Sisa
(Just a little further)

During a morning walk, I met a cattle herder on the road and started up a conversation.

Avy aiza ianareo? (Where have you come from?)

Bakao...... (Over there.) He answered in his local dialect and motioned with a pointed finger.

Oviana lasa ianareo? (When did you leave your village?)

Heriny tamin' ny omaly. (A week ago yesterday......)

*Kely sisa. (*I encouraged him. *Just a little further.)*

He had been walking with his zebu for over a week, carrying only a stick, a small backpack and a *lamba*[99] around his shoulders. Some people travel light. With the cattle market just meters from our home, this cattle herder was almost there.

On the same walk, I followed a young woman's footprint. Stepping my imprint in hers, I realized she impressed my heart. My stride fit hers. I had an epiphany moment. Telling a woman's story is what I am made for. I'm a voice for the voiceless.

Kely sisa. My life journey in Madagascar was just a little further. I had come far. I would leave this land but it's people would always be held in my heart.

One day you may have an epiphany moment. Seeing your life flash before you, is it something you want to watch?

The Paris Opera House sits on three acres of land, its interior constructed so that four-fifths of its theater is the backstage.[100] The backstage design ensures the onstage success. As I walked,

I felt that my thirty years on the mission field was four-fifths of my backstage, a springboard, giving me wings to fly.

"I am, because we are, and since we are, I am,"[101] expresses African theologian John Mbiti. We are not meant to live alone but rather in community, rubbing shoulders, engaged in one another's lives. Intricately created by God, we need each other.

Interdependent on one another, some of us are on stage, some back stage and others in the audience. Together, we are the church. Together, we live a life that matters.

Flat Tires

During our final few months of living in Madagascar, I had a dream.

> *Todd and I are bike riding in the middle of nothing. Cacti, thorn trees and sand are all around. How we ever got here on this sandy trek, bike riding, I don't know. This location isn't really conducive to riding a bike.*

> *In the middle of the desert, we find ourselves in a predicament. Both having flat tires, there is not a building or a person around. There is no help in sight. We are out of ideas – out of options. Sitting on the side of the dirt trek in silence, we ponder our predicament.*

> *We glance up into the glaring sunlight. Shocked at the sight, we realize, here comes Jesus! Laughing, skipping down the road, coming closer - headed our way!*

And Jesus is not alone. He is with a whole group of people chatting, celebrating, laughing, too!

Walking as a group, they are carrying all kinds of supplies. Compassionate friends with tarps to protect us from the hot sun and picnic baskets balanced on top of their heads filled with delicious gourmet foods from exotic lands. Others carry coolers filled with ice cold drinks for the hot journey while the musicians in the group sing as they walk, playing guitars, harps and stringed instruments. A whole symphony – bringing merriment and joy.

And in the midst of the crowd... is Jesus, carrying the bicycle pump. And by his side, are his disciples, carrying new tires. Life is a celebration. It's a party!

Life may bring us to mysterious places. Circumstances can propel us on a two-wheel balancing act right into the middle of the desert. Accompanied by God into arduous challenges of life, hardship brings us to our knees humbling us, building character. Stuck and stranded without energy, ideas and options, we trust in God and one another.

Just when our tires are flat, Jesus shows up, carrying the tire pump, celebrating and bringing a party. Despair is a part of life's journey. Although uncertain of our way forward, Jesus, as our best friend, knows how to lift us up and out of the desert, taking us home, filling our hearts with rejoicing, worship, song and dance.

Having times of discouragement? Turn to prayer.
Just about to quit? Turn to prayer.
Stressed out and worried? Jesus makes the difference,
bringing a host of followers to join in the celebration.

God is Everywhere

Spiritual journeys are all about lifestyle. Jesus invites us to live with him 24 hours a day, dwelling among us, desiring us to draw near. Embracing us with love, God is everywhere. Touching his cloak and dining with him, our personal spiritual health solidifies with loving community. Strong relational health recognizes that growth is not only an individual endeavor but also a community adventure.

Sharing our faith is part of our spiritual wellbeing. It's true connection. With a healthy, vibrant community of believers, people experience awareness of God. Epiphanies remind us that God is active in our everyday lives and we begin to share our story. Stories impact and increase our faith. Evangelism takes place naturally. With joy-filled, good-news communicated intimately, person-to-person, moments of life become thin, sacred, holy spaces.

Winston Churchill said, "There is no doubt that it is around the family and the home that all the greatest virtues, the most dominating virtues of human society, are created, strengthened and maintained."[102] Family and community open us to understand one another's needs. The best place for us to learn compassion and encouragement is in the heart of a good home and community.

African worldview reminds us; God is everywhere. General African Traditional Religion believes that god is in all places. Christians call this *omnipresence*. A deep belief system in African Traditional Religion is the foundation that god is present and the spirit is everywhere, in the trees, water, animals, etc. This belief system deeply entrenches the African's daily life and is supported by the community, establishing the groundwork for people to be receptive to Christianity.

At the heart of the Malagasy culture is the belief that *Zanahary* (the Malagasy name for God) is the provider and creator of everything present. God's provision is the core of their culture and they bless *Zanahary* for providing their needs. The influence of community and respect for elders supports this faith. Belief in God is still very evident.

With a strong sense of community influencing their way of life, the Malagasy live in multi-generational communities. This cultural structure organically strengthens the body of Christ, making the community ready to serve God, giving practical opportunity for connecting with others. Elders are role models, passing on wisdom from generation to generation, leaving a legacy of love.

Together

In Madagascar, life is lived together. Most tasks are done with others, in community – washing clothes, tilling rice fields, cooking, going to the market, even bathing in the river. Communal lifestyle is a powerful life tool. *Miaraka* is the word the Malagasy use to express this gift of togetherness.

Groups, schools, and teams traveling from various countries have been blessed to partake in the welcoming Malagasy hospitality while visiting this unique and picturesque island. Taking part in one another's lives and seeing the beauty of this magical island, groups and individuals comfort crying babies and hold a child's hand. Loving somebody from an extremely different culture challenges us to leave behind a learned way of thinking and embrace the lifestyle of another.

Spiritual growth occurs while walking in another's shoes. Malagasy friends have welcomed and appreciated visitors of all sorts. Active, loving engagement with one another challenges the community to think in another's thought pattern, understand another world-view, listen to questions and feel one another's burdens.

Focusing on similarities rather than differences, life is enhanced. Looking at life through the prism of the Holy Scripture, our starting point is the Word of God. Scriptures are the plumb-line. The beloved community evolves around loving one another as we love God and ourselves.

Living in harmony with others is not always easy, but it is empowering. Strengthening God's people, we reach out and take a hand. As a community, we grow in love with others, sharing faith-stories. Through the hope of the Gospel, we offer a bridge to people from different lands. With Christian integrity and living transparent, obedient lives, we pray our witness will encourage holy character and vibrant, self-sustaining ministry.

Living side-by-side with those of another culture is often called cross-fertilization. There is a blend, a melding, a mixing of ideas and customs from a myriad of traditions. With healthy exchange, this interchange involves a willingness to learn from one another. In a process of give and take, openness produces enrichment of one another's ideas and experiences and respect of one another's cultural and contextual peculiarities.

The Malagasy have blessed our family and friends who have traveled across oceans to experience life in Madagascar. Humble to the core, the Malagasy are unpretentious. Impoverished life is basic, simple, lived on the land. In Madagascar, people are not expecting what might be called an 'ideal life.' Embracing the sweet and the bitter, they welcome what life offers. With assistance from family and friends, multi-generational communities help bear the pain.

Many visitors have opened their hearts and financial treasures to assist the Malagasy with famine relief, health care, jobs and educational scholarships. Schools, churches (cathedrals!) and health clinics have been built. Lives have been touched, transformed. This co-mingling of lives, this Miaraka *togetherness*, this spiritual life-exchange, is what we call People Reaching People. Called to go forth into the world by the power of the Spirit, we put a cross in our pocket, reminding us that God is with us, everywhere, all the time.

Come and See

Cultural anthropologists remind Americans that we are some of the most individualistic people in the world. It is one of the few cultures, for example, where young people leave

126

home, select a mate, and then inform their parents. This cultural mindset has its own set of strengths and weaknesses. Individualism encourages self-initiative and acceptance of responsibility. But faith can become too private, individualistic and self-centered. Such practices wilt mustard seeds of faith.

Influence of a short-term mission to another country can carry over long after the visit. Inviting people to come and see what God is doing around the world breeds opportunity for personalizing involvement in global partnership, giving wings for witness at home and abroad. Experiencing faith in another culture with relational unity and community through love and compassion in the Lord Jesus Christ helps one another work through conflict. When God's people live transparent lives filled with integrity, the church is on the move.

While writing the first draft of this final memoir of our life in Madagascar in Toliara, my husband Todd received the following email.

Dear Bishop,

I was not sure if your departure from Madagascar was still on track with the virus and all, and I just received "*Veloma*, Madagascar" from People Reaching People. So, you and Patsy are indeed off to embark on the next "season" of Kingdom service.

I am sure this is a busy time and you probably do not need one more e-mail to read, but I did want to once again express what a joy it was to spend time with you and the Malagasy people in Madagascar. That experience reshaped my spiritual journey, and I am a better Christian today than when we first met. My personal relationship with Jesus was transformed in Madagascar by being a part of the Malagasy's enthusiasm for Jesus, and your hospitality in showing how God was working in the Diocese of Toliara. Your kindness and willingness to allow me to be a part of God's work in the Diocese, opened the door for me to realize that I can have a bigger part to play in Kingdom building, that God wants me to be a part of His plan.

I read that you will continue to be in partnership with SAMS. You have my e-mail, if you would keep in touch and let me know of your next "adventure," Marianne and I will continue to pray and support you and Patsy.

With love,
God's Peace,
Ken and Marianne

Spiritual friendships nurture the development of one another's soul. Love translates a desire to help each other become all they were intended to be. Offering the gift of ourselves to one another and walking in companionship on the journey of life, we become the fullness of God's beloved community.

Even when extremes of culture and economic diversity are evident, global Christians can partake in life together, loving one another as God would love us. Partnership between the poverty-stricken Malagasy and the western church can be quite complicated. A Malagasy evangelist earns the equivalent of $35 USD per month and a priest earns $75 USD per month. This amount can be a dinner for two in a nice but not even necessarily upscale restaurant in many parts of the United States.

"What really raises one's indignation about suffering is not suffering intrinsically but the senselessness of suffering."[103] The difficulty of much of the suffering in Madagascar is that it seems senseless and could be assisted by partners in mission. Because it's made my heart break, I ask myself, imploring others to do the same. *How can we help?*

The Applause of Heaven

The world tells us a lie that eats away like a termite of the soul. It goes something like this; "Confidence will make you selfish." We fear becoming prideful, thinking subconsciously we will forget others and only pursue our own agendas. But here's a beautiful secret from Jesus. True confidence leads to service.

Insecurity turns us inward, causing us to focus on ourselves. But confidence and courage bring security, allowing us to serve others in joyful freedom and peace. Hearing from God takes thought, insight and prayerful intentionality.

What would it be like to hear applause from heaven? Would it be easy for you to hear, knowing *that* applause was meant for you? How would you react? Uneasy? Do you feel too self-conscious or unworthy to accept the attention?

The truth is, when God thinks of you, he smiles. Grinning ear-to-ear, love swells in his heart. "God bursts with love for humans."[104] With a welcoming embrace, God is emotionally involved with his creation –human beings.

Thinking God may be applauding for me causes a bit of welcomed surprise. Bewildered and baffled, I silently wonder. *Really? Could God be clapping for me?* And yet, when I really consider his handiwork and workmanship, I think God *does* clap for each of us. The Creator is pleased with his creation. God is obviously thrilled with His work; why is it so hard to embrace this applause from heaven?

When we are quietly confident in who God is and who we are in relationship with God, life is a celebration and we scatter joy. Service becomes a delight. Confidently

knowing we are made in the image of God, our identities are based upon truth, and we have the joy of a clearer perspective.

What happens when we combine courage, connection, confidence and meaning with the world of work? Like putting a conch shell to the ear and hearing the ocean, I think we may hear the applause of heaven.

Blessed to Be a Blessing

As we were packing up to leave Madagascar a final time, we spent an afternoon organizing the Resource Center and Library on the compound. Realizing that we needed to carry boxes of books we would be leaving behind from the Gathering Place, a friend suggested we enlist two little boys about 6 and 8 years old to help. I was doubtful they could actually be of assistance, but she was certain! These two young comrade neighbors at the Cathedral Complex seemed to always be looking for some-thing to do and were quite open to being helpful.

So, we enlisted the children's service, dampened two wash-cloths with bleach water and gave them the task of wiping down all the books. Dust and dirt are hard to conquer in Madagascar and our little friends were energetically helpful with their masks on and hands washed.

Even though COVID-19 was a continued threat, social dis-tancing flew out the window. At one point I admonished my friend to keep a distance, as the virus still hovered over the country and neighboring village, but finally gave up and called upon the canopy of the Holy Spirit to protect us all, and espe-cially my friend since she was in the midst of these two boys whose masks kept slipping. At the end of the day, she invoked Jesus' blessing that through their lives they would attack other projects as energetically and completely as they had this one.

Courageously, we make every effort to accept our calling and the life God has assigned. Like Paul, we learn the secret of being content in any and every situation, whether well fed or hungry, whether living in plenty or in want, being exposed to disease or not, we invoke Jesus' blessing.[105] As a child of the King, we live bravely, confidently, securely, graciously, gratefully.

Thankfully, we can gather a support system to coach us through the difficult periods of time as we look to the future ahead. Our family is grateful to many individuals; mentors, professional counselors, friends, prayer warriors and even little children who walked this journey with us. Especially we are indebted to our People Reaching People leadership team, supporters, donors and our Malagasy friends who have worked together, held hands, and carried one another's burdens.

As he was dying, Dad was a profound example of gratitude. To the very end he expressed appreciation to those who visited, for those he loved and for those who cared for him. He said "Thank You" constantly; it could have been the last words he ever spoke. He was grateful even when my sister Betsy and I nervously cared for him and forgot to open the lid on the portable urinal and he peed all over the bed. Finally, full of transparency and without any shame, he blessed us, laughing at the incident.

The Hebrew word in the Old Testament for bless is *barakh*, meaning to bend the knee. "When we bless God or others, we are in essence bringing a gift on bended knee."[106] When Malagasy ask one another for forgiveness, it is part of the culture to kneel at the feet of those whom they offended. This humility, part of their inborn identity, is imparted to others.

The Malagasy have taught us many things. Most of all, they have blessed us. By God's grace, we hope to have also taught them. It's been a win-win situation, blessed to be a blessing.

We Make a Life by What We Give

Driving around Southern Madagascar on roads that make teeth rattle and eyeballs jiggle has been quite exhausting. It's hard, grueling really, to continually speak in a foreign tongue, preaching, teaching and communicating daily in a second language.

Some people have asked me, "Why have you and Todd stayed for so long and done this type of work when it is so difficult?"

Love inspires our motivation for living. Love settles us down and begins extending mercy to those around us. As Winston Churchill observed, "We make a living by what we get. We make a life by what we give."[107]

When I get to heaven, I anticipate the pleasure of walking into the open arms of God giving me a spine-crushing hug. I am pleased with our teamwork and what has been accomplished for the Lord and His Kingdom. We have been given the privilege of serving Christ.[108] We have done our best, run the full distance, kept the faith...and now a victory prize is awaiting.

Packing up the last odds and ends preparing to leave Madagascar, my husband discovered a metal cup for his toothbrush on the bathroom sink. It is engraved as the second prizewinner for a golf tournament in Limuru, Kenya.

Holding it high in the air, he exclaimed, "We can't leave this behind!"

"Really? You want to take that?" I incredulously replied.

"Yes! I won this!" Like a little boy, my husband was so proud of his trophy.

In reality, we all have a prize awaiting. When we have finished our race and come to the end of our time, God is waiting to present us with our victory prize—a prize for being in right relationship with God.[109]

Ultimately, that is what life is all about. It's not about how many buildings have been constructed, how many churches have been planted or even the number of souls who have come to know Christ. Our legacy, this victory prize, only comes from being in right relationship with God. That's why God gives us that applause of heaven ...because we are his friend and we are in right relationship with him.

Coming back from a walk with my husband, I kissed him. *"Thank you, Sweetie. I enjoyed it. I would not have done it without you."* A brain light bulb switched on and I thought, *Hmmm. This so describes my life in Madagascar.*

Most likely, I would have never come to Madagascar if it weren't for my husband's original call to go as a missionary to this unique island. *Thank you, Sweetie. I enjoyed it. I wouldn't have done it without you.*

"If the only prayer you say your whole life is *Thank You*, that would suffice."[110]

To all our friends, co-workers, partners and supporters around the globe who have been holding our hands and walking along-side us on the journey... *Thank you. I enjoyed it. I wouldn't have done it without you.*

Love Keeps Moving Forward

Love keeps moving forward. Motivating us through life, our guidebook of love and roadmap of life is found in 1 Corinthians 13. Love is patient, love is kind, love is not jealous.[111] Love is the essence of who we are.

The experience and challenge of loving others in all situations and in all conditions is a lifelong journey. Love doesn't expire. It doesn't have an expatriation date. Love does not evaporate when we fly to another country. Love continues beyond borders.

"Where you go, I will go, and where you lodge, I will lodge. Your people shall be my people, and your God, my God."[112] I said this to my husband when we first went to Madagascar, and in the process of thirty years, the Malagasy people have become my people and the sharing of our faith has become their God. True friends, remain friends for life. Love keeps moving forward.

As we said goodbye to our Malagasy friends, we knew then, as we still know now, we will carry their loving faces *always* in our hearts. While we were on the mission field, I called Madagascar, the forgotten island. All kinds of aid and relief programs are directed throughout Africa, but Madagascar, especially the southern region, was forgotten.

I would like to think that it is now not as forgotten as it once was. To the many people who have traveled with us on our journey and for those who continue to play a role in the lives of the Malagasy people, thank you. We appreciate you taking this journey with us, as People Reaching People. Love keeps moving forward.

The Suitcase of Our Heart

Sometimes, love is a dare. Living in Madagascar, for me, was a love dare, a journey of challenge and love. Love doesn't wobble when things don't go the way you want them to be. Love is steady, forgiving, trusting.

Love doesn't quit when hardships come. Love endures drought, famine, discrimination, inconveniences, and difficulty. Love calls us to listen, patiently remembering sorrows and sweetness. Love encourages, bringing a smile to another's face.

Love calls us to dream, think big, and work hard. Love is not left behind at the airport but is packed away in the suitcase of our heart. Our deepest recess, love travels with us wherever we go. Love is the way, the truth and the life.

Love endures the unpredictable because ultimate love dares in all circumstances. Love does not hesitate but gives fully – every ounce, down to the last drop. Love surrenders. Like the widow who only had two small coins, love gives everything she has.

It's not what we *do* for the Lord that matters--it's how we love. Life is a communal effort, practiced daily. Life begins and ends with love, not on its own accord, but because of the unending, never failing, always trusting love – only the love of God is carried with us, in the suitcase of our hearts.

Fly!!!

The most important thing that parents can teach their children is how to get along without them. [113]

And now, as I come to the end of our full-time, missionary story, my fingers freeze. Not physically, because as I write this last entry, it is summer in Madagascar. Sweating profusely, it's 94 degrees outside and just a few degrees less in the house. But emotionally, the sinews and tendons fail to dance on the keyboard as they have with other writings. More like fingers of an old woman pained with arthritis, joints feel inflamed. I want to skip this transitional chapter of life.

With few days remaining, Todd and I are saying goodbye to a country and its people with whom we have lived almost three decades. Embracing us as their own, the Malagasy people have caused us to become *tamana*, at home, in a place I thought I never could settle, much less be changed by.

When I first moved to Toliara, I wrote myself a question on a blue 4x6 index card. Are you strong enough to live in Toliara and perform all the duties and responsibilities of a Bishop's wife and a woman priest in a new Diocese that you, your husband and your team will start from ground zero?

I guess by the grace of God, I have found that answer. When I think of the wisdom and scope of God's plan, I fall to my knees and pray to the Father, the Creator of everything in heaven and on earth. I see from his glorious, unlimited resources, he gives mighty inner strength through his Holy Spirit. My heart is at home as I trust him.

For me, Madagascar has been my landscape, my frame of reference, a picture frame for life. It has been the way through which I have woven my tapestry and perceived the world. Living in Madagascar has given me new eyes. It's been the *window of my soul.*

Change is difficult. Flying from point A to point B, we tend to want to skip the hard part, getting quickly to the destination. But life does not always offer comfort. We have the necessity of packing and lugging heavy suitcases, along with the weary journey and clumsiness of passing through metal detectors and security checks.

Even more unsettling are goodbyes, uncertainties, and uncomfortable emotions along the way. Specifically at the time of our leaving, the COVID-19 pandemic stretched our elastically. Tired, weary and forced to say goodbye with the pandemic at our doorstep, normal ceremonies were cancelled, loved ones not able to visit. After thirty years of living with the Malagasy people, sadly, we left without giving a handshake or a hug. But we gave every part of ourselves.

Martin Luther King, Jr. said, "If you can't fly, then run. If you can't run, then walk. If you can't walk, crawl, but whatever you do, you have to keep moving forward."[114]

Opportunities for
Personal Reflection

Is there something you have done in life that you thought you would not enjoy but ended up truly appreciating?

How have you experienced love in unexpected places?

How have you passed on this love to surprise others?

Madagascar...
The Window of My Soull

T here is a difference between moving on and moving forward. Moving on seems to infer leaving behind what has been in the past and just go on. Moving forward not only looks ahead, but also learns from the past, offering hope, encouragement, growth and change. I like the idea of moving forward.

Chameleons have an uncanny ability of diverting their eyes in many directions and still clamping onto the branch beneath their limbs, moving forward. Looking back with hindsight while looking forward with forethought is sometimes exactly what we are called to do.

A Malagasy proverb reminds us. *Manao dian-tanalahy, jerena ny aloha, todihina ny aoriana.* "Travel like the chameleon, focusing forward, looking backward."[115]

After 30 years of missionary service and over 14 years of working in the Diocese of Toliara, the Lord has called us to return to the United States. Our years overseas have formed us into global Christians, providing ministry and purpose. Our sadness of leaving Madagascar is coupled with satisfaction as we see what the Lord has done.

In our years of missionary service, we have formed over 150 church communities, shared the Good News of Jesus Christ with tens of thousands, provided jobs and economic development for multitudes, built over 11 healthcare clinics, sponsored the education of hundreds of children, formed church leaders, distributed famine relief and emergency response supplies, written a musical, built three evangelism schools, two cathedrals, and three primary schools.

Similar to life and our own children, ministry grows up. We wait so eagerly for our young ones to take their first steps... to experience life, to go off to college and pursue their dreams. Childhood is behind, and now our children step into the world and forge their own path in life. With hope, they follow our teachings. They strive, thrive, and bloom all on their own. The feeling is both overwhelmingly exciting yet heartbreaking at the same time. For as much as we want to always hold our children close, the time comes to let them spread their wings and fly.

The impact of our ministry would not have been made possible without our Heavenly Father and our supporters. All praise to an amazing God! We gratefully thank Him for allowing us to participate in His Kingdom with such amazing experiences and opportunity. We are also grateful to God for our amazing supporters, for hours of your steadfast prayers, for days of traveling across oceans to witness and participate in God's work, and for monetary support even when you had limited funds yourself. You have helped make possible what seemed impossible.

In the midst of a teary transition, we believe the Lord has great plans for our future. A few months after our arrival in the USA, I began serving as the Director of Spiritual Formation at St. Mary's Episcopal Church, in Stuart, Florida. Focusing on multigenerational spiritual growth at a vibrant church is a wonderful ministry match for me. At this time of writing, Todd continues to be a full time SAMS missionary using his years of experience to encourage global missions and missionary service, focusing on teaching and training in church planting, evangelism, and discipleship.

I don't think I will ever fully leave Madagascar. A piece of our hearts will always be with our friends on the Red Island and in the spiny desert of the Diocese of Toliara.

Oliver Wendell Holmes wrote, "Where we love is home. Home that our feet may leave, but not our hearts."[116]

We waited so eagerly for our children to take their first steps... to experience life, to go off to college and pursue their dreams. Childhood is behind, and now our children are stepping into the world to forge their own path in life, following God's teachings, striving, thriving, and blooming. The most important thing that parents can teach their children is how to get along without them.[117] When they accomplish this, the feeling is both overwhelming excitement and heartbreak at the same time. For as much as you want to always hold your children close, the time comes to let go and let them fly.

God gives...
A rainbow for every storm
A smile for every tear
A promise for every worry
A blessing for every hardship
A friend for every journey
A song for every heaviness
Strength for every weakness
An answer for every prayer.

Timeline

Selected Events 2012-2020
Madagascar: The Window of My Soul

2012		
	August	Patsy accepts the invitation from the Archbishop of the Indian Ocean to pioneer women's ministry as the first woman priest in the Anglican Church of Mauritius
	September	Patsy installed as first woman priest in the Anglican Diocese of Mauritius
	December	Patsy recognized as one of the most influential women of 2012 in the country of Mauritius (L'Express Newspaper)
2013		
	February	Todd elected 1st Diocesan Bishop of Toliara, at St. Lioka Malagasy Episcopal Church, Ankilifaly, Madagascar
		Cylone Haruna directly hits Toliara and a major part of the new Diocese of Toliara is damaged
		Patsy, back in Madagascar on a short trip for the election and delayed due to the hurricane, goes back to Mauritius. While airborne, she chicken-scratches words for *I'm Praying For You* on a small Air Madagascar airplane napkin.

March		Patsy meets Desmond Tutu for the first time
April		Todd enthroned as 1st Diocesan Bishop of Toliara, at St. Lioka Malagasy Episcopal Church, Ankilifaly, Madagascar
August		Collette Maurel and Patsy record 31 songs with Collette's brother and sister who flew in from South Africa for Collette's birthday
September		Storyline appears for *Miaraka: A Time to Dance* Musical
November		Auditions for *Miaraka: A Time to Dance* performers are held in Mauritius just before Patsy returns to live in Andranomena, Toliara, Madagascar
		Patsy and Collette record 14 songs (joined by Karl Brasse) on a new CD called *We Dance Therefore We Are*
2014		
April		Miaraka Foundation created, based in Mauritius
May-June		*Miaraka: A Time to Dance* Musical has their first performance at the IGCIC in Mauritius
June		Groundbreaking for St. Patrick's Cathedral
August		Mahaboboka School Dedicated
2015		
February		Tea with Archbishop Desmond Tutu, Capetown, South Africa

April	Todd and Patsy travel back to USA to visit churches in Southeast Florida. Collette joins then and they speak/sing at church teas to raise money in support of the Women's Center in Toliara	
August	At the invitation of Archbishop Desmond Tutu, Patsy and the *Miaraka: A Time to Dance* Mauritius Team travels for performances at the Cape Peninsula University for Technology for National Women's Day in South Africa.	
November	Performance of *Miaraka* songs for a Women's Conference at Sugar Beach Hotel, Mauritius	
2016		
February	Building of the Labyrinth, Church of the Good Shepherd, Tequesta, FL	
March	Dedication of St. Patrick's Cathedral, *Miaraka: A Time to Dance (Ny Andro Andohizana)* Performance in Toliara	
August	Women's ordination unanimously approved at Diocesan Synod of Toliara	
August	Women's Center dedicated to promote empowerment of women	
September	*Miaraka: A Time to Dance* Performance, St. Gregory's Episcopal Church, Boca Raton, FL	
October	*Miaraka: A Time to Dance (Ny Andro Andihizana)* Performance, Veztival, Toliara, Madagascar	

2017		
	June/July	Patsy and Todd walk the Camino de Compostela and take a pilgrimage to Lindisfarne and Iona and meet Corbi and Joe Sandoe (Patsy and Todd's eldest daughter and son-in-law) in Israel.
	August	Performance of *Ny Andro Andihizana* at the National Youth Conference in Antsiranana, Madagascar (August 23-27th 2017)
	December	Miaraka Foundation represented by Diane Watkins and Collette Maurel give a talk at the Human Rights Symposium at the Middlesex University campus, Flic-en-Flac, Mauritius
2018		
	July	1st Guesthouse completed at St. Patrick's Cathedral Complex
	August	Rev. Nolavy Osoro was the first woman ordained as deacon in the Diocese of Toliara
	December	Patsy and Todd take a 4-month sabbatical in West Palm Beach, FL
2019		
	April	Patsy and Todd return to Madagascar after sabbatical
	June	Charese and Corbi (Patsy and Todd's daughter's) Joe and Jabin Sandoe (Corbi's family) travel to Madagascar, hike the Tsingy National Park, and say hello and goodbye to our Malagasy friends.

July	2nd Guesthouse completed at St. Patrick's Cathedral Complex
August	Patsy's girlfriends come to Toliara for Patsy's 60th birthday and for Nolavy Osoro's ordination into the priesthood.
December	Gerry W. Cox, Jr. (Patsy's father, known to many as PopPop) passes away on December 2nd.
2020	
March	COVID hits Madagascar, everything shuts down
	Patsy continues writing books: *Made in Blue/Little Steps/Dancing in the Sunlight/Window of My Soul*
December	McGregor's Farewell Service on Dec. 6th, Diocese of Toliara
December	McGregor's Farewell Service on Dec. 12th, Antananarivo
	Todd receives supreme honor from the Malagasy Government and becomes a Knight on Dec. 12th in Antananarivo.
	The Remi Rabenirina Family (3 generations) join us for a farewell dinner. This was very meaningful since Bishop Remi and his family met us at the airport on our first arrival to Madagascar in August 1991.
December	McGregor's Farewell from Madagascar, Dec. 15th

Study Guide

A thank you to Cindy Faye for creating this wonderful accompaniment to *Window of My Soul*

Chapter 1 - Courage

1. Describe a journey you've been on that has perhaps spanned months or years – where did it start and how have you adjusted or grown over that span of time? How did it change you? Others close to you?

2. Be strong and courageous. Do not be afraid; do not be discouraged, for the Lord your God will be with you wherever you go.[118] What does this scripture verse mean to you? How has it played out in your life or the life of another you may have observed?

3. Paul reminds us of this spiritual tug-of-war, telling us to be completely confident in the gospel.[119] God does the saving. We do the believing. God does the leading. We do the following. Response is our choice. Can you reflect on a time when you were in this type of spiritual tug-of-war –seeking to understand where God was leading you? How did you respond in that moment? How would you respond today?

4. "It's not what you do, it's why you do it that makes a difference."[120] What is driving some of the ministry work or other activities you may be involved in? What have your learned? What have you taught? Why has it worked? What has been meaningful? How have you been blessed?

5. Where can you worship-walk more slowly? More bravely? More confidently?

6. "I needed God to refresh my perspective and remind me, it *is* a wonderful world. I needed a divine reversal." Is there a place in your life right now that you are struggling? An area that needs refined, reversed or rewritten? An area for God to intervene and show His presence to you?

7. Courageously, we make every effort to accept our calling and the life God has assigned. Like Paul, we learn the secret of being content in any and every situation, whether well fed or hungry, whether living in plenty or in want.[121] As a child of the King, we live bravely, confidently and securely. In what ways have you found to be content in your life's situations? What have been sometimes you have experience moments of plenty/periods of want? How have you responded? How can you respond more bravely, confidently or securely today? In the future? How will this scripture help anchor you? Your family?

Chapter 2 - Calling

1. Like Reese, perhaps it would be easiest to receive a call from Harold Finch, reminding us who we are and no matter our circumstances, we are made for a purpose. Each one of us has a call to use our talents to the glory of God in service to one another. God is the One who is leading us on the road of life, calling us to reach out and be of assistance to our communities.

2. Have you struggled to understand your calling or purpose? How you are being called out to be of assistance to your community?

    What do you feel is your calling today? How are you living that out?

3. One definition of leader is "anyone who takes responsibility for finding the potential in people and processes, and who has the courage to develop that potential."[122] Where do you see leaders in your life today? In what ways are you called to lead others, to build into them and develop their potential?

4. Scripture calls us living epistles. No matter what culture we live in, our lives are to be testimonies to God's goodness and grace. With Scripture as our plumb line to measure truth, we can live into our calling, because God has called us.[123] Have you seen others living in their calling/their purpose? What about you? Have you taken a small first step to seek that direction?

5. Sometimes the question of considering our calling is simple. Instead of searching for the burning bush, maybe God is just asking, "Are you willing?" Are we willing? What may be holding you back? How do you feel about God calling YOU? Are you listening?

6. Four simple guidelines remind us that calling doesn't have to be complicated. Sometimes, we just start where we are, in our present situation.

   - Awareness of need. Certainly, there was need in Madagascar. I still call it the forgotten island. What is the awareness of need near you?
   - Who is calling? Are we listening?
   - Why not? When we believe we have a calling, the calling will be tested. Put it in the positive. Why wouldn't God call me?
   - Obedience. Will we follow?

7. God has called each one of us. Our callings are unique. How do you live into your calling? How do you hold your own cup?

8. Basically, as Todd and I lived out our callings, we focused on three things:
   1) Pray. God is the center.
   2) Observe what God is doing, and do that.
   3) Make disciples. Build relationships.
      How can we apply these principles to our daily lives? God has called each one of us. Our callings are unique. How do you live into your calling? How do you hold your own cup?

Chapter 3 Character

1. Humility soaks situations in prayer. It is a great temptation to do the work of the Lord with energy and gumption. However, if we activate without soaking prayer, we may spin wheels for God with great momentum, but without going anywhere. How can we approach situations in prayer? How might a situation have turned out better if it was basked in prayer first?

2. Henri Nouwen writes of "hospitality of the heart." Hospitality at its core is the opening of the heart. Opening our hearts means gathering others in. In what ways can we practice hospitality more generously? Where can we greet and invite others into our lives? Our homes? Our churches or ministry?

3. The Malagasy version of the Beatitudes writes, "Blessed are they who realize their need for God..."

   How does this resonate for you? In what ways can we live out this "Malagasy Beatitude"? How can we apply this to our culture/our community?

4. This idea of poor in spirit portrays realization of our utter helplessness and the need to put our whole trust in God. Where is your trust in God today? Where do you place your trust?

5. What if we had the vision to see every person in our life as someone to serve, someone to whom we 'tip our hat'? What if our first response was the desire to be kind, to be

of service the way Jesus was? Think about this past week – where have you had the opportunity to be kind, to be of service as Jesus served?

6. "From the moment you close your Bible in the morning, nearly everything else you'll encounter throughout the day will be luring you away from its truths. The opinions of your coworkers, the news coverage on television, your typical web sites, the various temptations of the day – all of these and more will be working overtime to shape your perceptions of what's true and most desirable in life."[124] How can we stay more grounded in The Word? How can we alter our priorities each day to stay tuned to God's purposes and principles in our lives?

7. Everyone needs wise counsel throughout life. Wise people pursue it and gladly receive it. It is essential to seek godly advice, healthy friendships and experienced mentors. Interlocking the roots of truth with another's helpful support allows us to face problems and stand strong. Where do I find my counsel? How can I stay connected to godly community and build mentoring relationships?

Chapter 4 Chemistry

1. Think about a group you've been part of that struggled to work well together. Did any members of the group feel unaccepted? If so, how did that affect the team dynamics?

2. Creation brings us into special relationship with God. How we treat ourselves matters. I realize (and admit) I am way too hard on myself, and others. God calls me "very good."[125]

Why do I have trouble calling myself that? How can you encourage others to be less hard on themselves, especially in ministry?

3. Growing strong requires seeking the Lord through his word as well as spending time with an older and stronger Christian through discipleship. We need one another. Where are you spending time with other Christians to develop your Christian walk more fully? Are there others you could mentor now, too?

4. Negative thought patterns gradually grow weaker and weaker and the lights stay connected. Have you found triggers that bring you to negative thoughts or emotions? Can you acknowledge these triggers ahead of time? What are ways that you can gradually grow in this area?

5. But God promises to be our constant companion, caring for us, protecting us every step of our journey. It is important to remember we are being raised as a warrior, not as a sofa-sitting Christian. How do you reflect the heart and character of a warrior? Do you know what "your sword" is? How/when do you put it to use?

6. Designed to be in the battle, it's important to be spiritually fit, confident, equipped for the fight with God at the helm. Having this attitude is critical to our mind-set. When trials enter our lives, we will be armed, not alarmed. Until we reach our ultimate home in heaven, we will be at war. How can you better train to be a warrior for Christ? What tools or training do you need today?

7. "Fear not, for I am with you: Be not dismayed, for I am your God. I will strengthen you. Yes, I will help you. I will uphold you with my righteous right hand."[126] "Teach these great truths to trustworthy people who are able to pass them on to others."[127] When people live in community, there is an opportunity to naturally share faith and disciple one another. Are you brave enough to be a warrior? What warrior-like qualities can you build up today? In what other areas do you want to explore more training?

Chapter 5 Competency

1. As we teach discipleship, we emphasize, "Just teach what you know." Where may it be that you are being called to greater discipleship? Perhaps to teach? Has God knocked at your heart? How did you respond?

2. When choosing disciples, find a person strong in the 3 T's: Time, Trust and Teachability. Building relationships takes time. Do they have enough time to be a disciple? Do they trust you? Are they teachable? Spending time with the person will help you decide if they are up to the challenge of being a role model to others.

3. My husband says, "*The church is to be a place where we are changed.*"[128] Let's be a part of that change, by hydrating ourselves spiritually and cultivating the soil for God to work within us as we lean on, trust in, and are confident in the Lord with all our hearts and minds.[129] What is the source of your spiritual hydration?

4. Transformation of mind, body, soul and spirit takes dedication and commitment. The Diocese of Toliara focuses on six disciplines: Daily devotions, Discipleship, Evangelism, Giving, Fasting and Obedience to God and the Scriptures. Friendship with God is not a series of religious duties but rather a relationship. Are there disciplines you do regularly? How have these disciplines impacted you? Your family? Any other of the disciplines you'd like to explore more fully?

5. What are the gifts that God has given you? Are you developing them? Are you using them? Are you sharing them? Are you teaching what you know?

6. Leaders are responsible to make sure that all believers are equipped for ministry. God's will for every believer is spiritual maturity and God calls all believers to minister to the world and the church. Service in the body of Christ isn't limited to one's gender. In God's army, we've been drafted into service. Every Christian is created for ministry. It is part of our identity in Christ.

   Where have you experienced amazing Christian leadership? How have your leadership roles emerged or where would you like to grow in your leadership opportunities? Where have you been impacted by women in ministry or leadership?

7. Live out your calling, for you have been called by God.[130] When God calls us to a mission, that mission is open to all. Where are you being called in your mission? Your ministry? Your home or community to serve God and

others? Is God calling you? When have you been a torch lighter? A torch bearer?

Chapter 6 Community

1. I am, because we are, and since we are, I am," expresses African theologian John Mbiti. We are not meant to live alone but rather in community, rubbing shoulders, engaged in one another's lives. Intricately created by God, we need each other. Interdependent on one another, some of us are on stage, some back stage and others in the audience. Together, we are the church. Together, we live a life that matters. Describe the communities you are a part of today – family, neighbors, schools, church, your city, etc.

2. Cultural anthropologists remind Americans that we are some of the most individualistic people in the world. Individualism encourages self-initiative and acceptance of responsibility. But faith can become too private, individualistic, and self-centered. Such practices wilt mustard seeds of faith. How do these statements impact you? What has been your experience?

3. Thinking God may be applauding for me causes a bit of welcomed surprise. Bewildered and baffled, I silently wonder. *Really? Could God be clapping for me?* And yet, when I really consider his handiwork and workmanship, I think God *does* clap for each of us. The Creator is pleased with his creation. "God is obviously thrilled with His work; why is it so hard to embrace this applause from heaven?"

4. Love inspires our motivation for living. Love settles us down and begins extending mercy to those around us. As Winston Churchill observed, "We make a living by what we get. We make a life by what we give." Where are you able to give of yourself in service to others? How has that service impacted you?

5. Our legacy, this victory prize, only comes from being in right relationship with God. That's why God gives us that applause of heaven ...because we are his friend and we are in right relationship with him. How are you working to build into your relationship with Jesus? How do you view your homecoming with Him in heaven?

6. It's not what we do for the Lord that matters. It's how we love. Life is a communal effort, practiced daily. Life begins and ends with love, not on its own accord, but because of the unending, never failing, always trusting love – only the love of God is carried with us, in the suitcase of our hearts. With these final words, how can you love better, build more community and practice the Spiritual disciplines more fully? How are you called to more deeply love others?

7 "Travel like the chameleon, focusing forward, looking backward." What are your next steps? Where is God leading you today?

Acknowledgements

H ow can I say **Thank you!** to all the people who have touched my life in a myriad of ways? Supporters who allowed us to get to the mission field with generous financial contributions; friends and family, who in spite of thinking we were crazy, held our hands throughout our journey and even came to visit; the Malagasy people who gave me a new perspective for life – a new window to look out from – the window of my soul.

How can I thank my Eagle and Child writing team, Lynne Curtis, Bev Erasmus, Cindy Faye, Collette Maurel, Polly Montgomery and Beth Strickland for reading several rough drafts, reflecting on my writings and challenging me to go deeper, write from my heart, challenging me to get to the roots of my thoughts and feelings?

How do I thank the quarterback of this team, Emily Nell Lagerquist, who got stuck for 9 ½ months in Madagascar during the beginning of COVID-19 (God knew I needed her!) and spent endless hours talking, brainstorming, proofing, editing, documenting footnotes for this book and working with Joyce Fletcher on the publishing aspects of this memoir? The two of them worked relentlessly to get the book into publication.

How can I thank the women in my life from whom I have been encouraged, nurtured, challenged to be myself and follow little steps of walking into my God-given calling? Thank you especially to Cheryl Harman for providing beautiful photographs for the cover and interior of the book.

I would like to thank my husband for taking me into the mission field in the first place – even though I didn't *want* to – and for starting me on this journey of transformation from the inside out, and to my two daughters who allowed mom to be mom and loved me through the journey – potholes and all.

I thank the global church and the body of Christ – in its glory and its failures – for its foundational teachings and truth of the gospel – to have courage to walk into our callings with character, chemistry, competency, living in community, all to the glory of God.

Finally, I thank God, the author and perfector of my faith. I celebrate God and scatter joy. It does not need to be only the Christmas season that we exclaim,

"Joy to the world, the Lord is come. Come let us adore him!"

Appendix A

I n August 2012 I was invited by Archbishop Ian Ernest to serve as the parish priest of St. Simon's the Fisherman in Maurirtius for one year. This was a groundbreaking endeavor since there had never been a women clergy serving in Mauritius. The local news media became interested and wated to know more about the first woman priest. The local newspaper L'Express wrote an article about women in ministry, featuring an interview with me. That year (2012) I was recognized as one of the most influential women of the year in the country of Mauritius.

Article Published in Mauritius
Paper L'Express
September 22, 2012

The Rev. Patricia Cox McGregor:
"The woman priest brings a new sensibility
to the Church."
Translated from French

Tomorrow an historic event occurs for the Anglican Diocese of Mauritius with the installation of the first woman clergy. This idea made its way in the Province of the Indian Ocean since 2006 and the heads of the Church of England finally focused on their choice, Patricia Cox McGregor, of American origin and an ordained priest in 2006. She opens the pathway of priesthood for women in Mauritius. In an interview in

Mauritius last Wednesday with L'Express newspaper, the new Anglican clergywoman refuses to make a comparison between men and women priests but recognizes that it may provide a key in the affairs of the Church because of its sensitivity. This same sensitivity could help to "eliminate certain ambiguous situations and negative or detrimental images of the Church."

L'Express: What are the functions of a priest of the Anglican Church?

The Rev. Patricia McGregor: The functions of an Anglican priest, whether male or female, are the same. The role is to take care of parishioners who have been entrusted to them as a priest. This means feeding them the word of God, taking care of them like a mother who takes care of her children. The main task is to support them in their spiritual journey. This is done in different ways such as: preaching, presiding at the Eucharist, caring for youth groups, performing marriage counseling and supporting parishioners in other life issues. To accomplish these tasks, we must befriend our congregation and love others. We must also be able to fully give ourselves to what God has asked us to do.

L'Express: Since you have been ordained in 2006 you lived in Madagascar. Is this a request for you to come exercise your ministry now in Mauritius?

The Rev. Patricia McGregor: Last February, Archbishop Ian Ernest asked me to consider the proposal to come serve his Diocese in Mauritius. My first reaction was to say no because of the responsibilities of my husband who is a Bishop in Madagascar. Besides my own responsibilities within the church, I am next to him, supporting him in his mission. Since then, my husband and I have discussed this request and prayed together to know the plan of God. Just after Easter we came here for a week in order to meet Bishop Ernest and meet a few parishioners in Tamarin. As a result of that visit, I am convinced that this has been a great opportunity given to me to go further in my spiritual life. You know the challenges of balancing family life and other professional activities, social and religious. Since my two children aged 22 and 23 years have already completed university studies and started working, I thought I could respond to this call for Mauritius. I'm here alone only because my husband cannot leave his position as Bishop in Madagascar. I have been here since the second week of August.

L'Express: Did you know much about Mauritius before agreeing to come?

The Rev. Patricia McGregor: Not much. I came here for the first time with my family about twelve years ago. We came from Madagascar, and we were here mainly to relax. We did not have time to really explore the country and its people.

L'Express: It's been just a month since you have come to Mauritius. Have you adapted to the culture and your parish in Tamarin?

The Rev. Patricia McGregor: So far, they have been most generous accepting me even though I do not speak French. In Madagascar, I am fluent in Malagasy the official language of Madagascar, but not French. Since my time here, I have been learning a few Kreol words spoken in everyday life. Also, I have learned the names of some typical Mauritian dishes that are very tasty. The parishioners have been great in helping me integrate into the parish. I had the chance to introduce myself last week to the faithful congregation of the Catholic Church during a prayer ceremony at Black River. They applauded me as being a woman priest. It was very heart-warming.

L'Express: Do you feel comfortable in a male-dominated world of clergy?

The Rev. Patricia McGregor: I feel that I have the support of Archbishop Ian Ernest and all the clergy. I just want to be myself, to be the person God wants me to be and use all the talents and gifts he has given me to guide the parishioners of Tamarin. For me to be a priest should not be conditioned on the state of being a man or a woman, rather to live into the call of God. God has called us to a mission and that mission is open to all.

L'Express: And what is the attitude of your male colleagues to you?

The Rev. Patricia McGregor: (With a grin) From what I see, they accept my presence, and they are very welcoming. But I think we should ask the Archbishop this question.

L'Express: You are a priest for six years. What is the value of a woman in the priesthood?

The Rev. Patricia McGregor: Man and woman are made differently, and each has different talents to offer the world. A woman priest is not in competition with a fellow male priest. For example, there are certainly different qualities such as compassion, tenderness, beauty, nurturing. I do not say that a man is not capable of compassion, but women more often are more sensitive to certain issues and this feminine sensitivity can be an asset in the Church. I think the presence of men and women in the clergy in a balanced manner gives the Church its 'raison d' etre' and its fullness. In our advisory role there are often situations where it would be better if it is a woman rather than a man who is listening to a parishioner seeking advice. If this person is crying I can, for example, comfort her, put my hand on hers and take her in my arms. I can embrace her. But if a man does this gesture, this can lead to all sorts of interpretations that may affect his function as a priest. There are also questions that women better understand, and feel more comfortable talking to another woman. This understanding can facilitate the process of counseling and help to quickly find solutions to specific problems. Another area where women often bring a different touch is the area of beauty. We like to embellish things and make things beautiful around us.

L'Express: Could you give us a concrete example where this might make a difference?

The Rev. Patricia McGregor: Here is a small example that I experienced recently at St. Simon parish in Tamarin. The first thing I noticed when I arrived was that there was no banner to represent the congregation. Even though it is a new community and not yet a church, a banner would help to form an identify for the congregation. I proposed this to the parishioners and everyone was delighted. I wonder if a male priest would have thought of this first. It is not just a symbol. This gives a tone to parish life and it creates the right atmosphere in the church. Once it was completed, we all gathered around the banner. This created a sense of identity and wholeness which is very important in the life of the Church. For generations, women have always crated the atmosphere in their homes to give a taste of family life. And it's the same atmosphere of friendliness, warmth, hospitality that women priests are trying to create in the church.

L'Express: You are in a position of responsibility within the Church of England. Do you think that women in the world are equal to men when it comes to occupying senior professional positions?

The Rev. Patricia McGregor: The world today needs talented people regardless of their gender or their function. But I must admit that in many parts of the world, women are still waging a battle to be in positions of responsibility. Women who had the opportunity to develop academic qualifications and who are equipped to be in leadership roles must understand that they should not give up this kind of opportunity.

L'Express: There are deep differences of view regarding a woman becoming a bishop in the Anglican Church to the point that some in the Church of England have threatened to leave the church. Do you see yourself taking the role of a Bishop one day?

The Rev. Patricia McGregor: I know that in many dioceses in America, they have women as Bishops. For me, I have no plans for this function. One Bishop in the house is enough. More seriously, in fact it is not we who decide, let God do his work.

L'Express: There are emblematic women in the bible. Do they have a symbolic resonance? Do they inspire you in your role as a priest?

The Rev. Patricia McGregor: These characters are role models for all of us regardless of our positions in life. I confess that Esther in the Bible inspires me a lot. She was in a position that allowed her to save God's people. I do not think she would have done this if God had not placed her in a position to be called to this mission. I would add that the characteristics of a leader in the Church do not vary regardless of whether the person is a man or a woman. All those who are called to take responsibility in the Church must be role models in society and work collaboratively in the church community.

L'Express: How do you think the presence of women as clergy can help society?
The Rev. Patricia McGregor: I think our presence in positions of responsibility can promote a healthy environment and contribute to the smooth running of the Church. Women are mothers and naturally we have a lot to offer. We have been created to nurture. We have a strong love for people and I think we can offer that love to the church. By this I mean that a woman priest living her life as a woman, wife, mother and priest in all its fullness can sometimes help to eliminate some ambiguous situations and negative images of the Church.

L'Express: You are a pioneer in the Anglican priesthood in Mauritius. Do you think you will be able to work with the clergy of other Christian churches that are predominately male?
The Rev. Patricia McGregor: I do not think Archbishop Ian Ernest would have asked me to be here if I did not have the capacity and skills. Indeed, ecumenism is a part of our mission as priests. One of the keys to a positive working relationship is mutual respect, dignity and integrity.

L'Express: Do you have any immediate plans for the construction of this parish nascent?
The Rev. Patricia McGregor: I've only been here for a month and I do not want to impose anything. Of course, I have some

ideas for the development of this parish, but I have not discussed anything with Bishop Ernest. I am here to serve and the most important thing at the moment and which I have already mentioned is to help parishioners to strengthen their faith.

L'Express: Madagascar is almost an adopted country for you because you have been there since 1991, what are your feelings about the political crisis in that country?

The Rev. Patricia McGregor: The situation appears to be in a decline. I love Madagascar and its people and it makes me deeply hurt to see how chaotic the country is today. I want to cry. I feel sorry for the Malagasy. They are a great people and have a sense of hospitality and community spirit. Despite their precarious existence, they have a lot of love to give to others. Poverty in Madagascar and in the world saddens me.

L'Express: Father Jean-Maurice Labour (Vicar General of the Catholic Church), I express my personal opinion and not the official church. I welcome this initiative of the Anglican Church for having women in the priestly ministry. It must be recognized that women have the intellectual and spiritual capacities to take responsibility within the Church. Already women are within the Catholic Church, contributing to our communities and diocesan organization. They are the ones who take on more responsibilities. To my knowledge there are no obstacles theological, doctrinal or biblical for women's ordination. Cardinal Carlo Maria Martini, called a "progressive catholic icon" because of his reformist ideas – and just died – wrote a spiritual testament that the Catholic Church was behind 200 years in several areas, including the issue of access of married men and women to the priesthood. Like Martini, I hope that the Catholic

Church is seriously considering the possibility of access to the priesthood of married men and women.

L'Express: Archbishop Ian Ernest, Archbishop of the Indian Ocean, "Bringing this feminine flavor in our diocese" A woman enters the official Anglican clergy tomorrow. What motivated this approach that could be called historic Anglican Church in Mauritius? In many Anglican Dioceses around the world today, there are women priests. The Anglican Community in Mauritius live in effect Sunday (note: tomorrow) a milestone in the life of our Diocese. The decision to have women as priests emanates from a decision the Synod of the Province of the Indian Ocean made in 2006 and the Diocese of Mauritius in 2008. This decision to call Rev. Patsy was made after consultations for two years with the clergy and the faithful in our parishes. Everything was weighed to allow us to make a decision that will fulfill the diocesan life. We have taken into account the Anglican approach to the empowerment of women as well as the cultural aspects of our country. There is really no reason doctrinal, biblical and theological to prevent us from giving women the same responsibilities. And above all to be considered a candidate for ordination to the priesthood. We have seen in several Anglican provinces in the world, how the role of woman priests has given a new dimension to the life of the Church. It was time to bring this feminine flavor in our diocese. That is why, today, after much preparation, we are able to call a woman priest in our diocese.

L'Express: Why a foreigner?
Archbishop Ian Ernest: This is due to the context, as we have already said. In our diocese, women candidates are being

considered for ordination to deacon and priest in the years to come. Reverend Patricia McGregor is here for a specific period of time to share with us her experience, not only in relation to the priesthood, but also in other areas. Beyond the office of priest, she is here to work for the empowerment of women, to encourage them to take a more active part in the various ministries of our church. You asked earlier about the welcome she has received from our clergy. A few days ago, she attended the last meeting of the clergy, and she received a wonderful welcome!

L'Express: What will the ceremony be tomorrow since Patricia McGregor has been ordained for a few years?

Archbishop Ian Ernest: Tomorrow will be what we call the "Installation Ceremony" of a parish priest. As a Bishop, I give her the authority to share my pastoral responsibilities. I give her a license to exercise the episcopal ministry, but first she will make vows of obedience to her Bishop and her successors, as well as the constitution of the Diocese. This ceremony will take place at "Parish of St. Simon The Fisherman," which is a new parish in the village of Tamarin. This parish was formed just over a year ago and has no place to worship. We thank the Catholic Church, especially the parish of St. Benedict, for a place for us to hold services until the construction of the Church of St. Simon.

Portrait Express:

Patricia Cox McGregor started cultivating her love of sports in her early years. This love of sports was strengthened while in college and has been with her since. Tennis, volleyball, golf, hiking and walking are just some of the disciplines she practiced when she was young. She draws strength every day by practicing some form of sports, a quiet strength she brings to her family and church. Sports, she says elsewhere, is not inseparable from her faith in God and therefore, her commitments within the Church. It is the same for music, her other passion. L'Express surprised her Wednesday afternoon with her guitar in hand surrounded by a dozen children as she was teaching them a sing linking sweetness and harmony. But this is not all, because Patricia Cox McGregor has yet another strong arrow in her bow: writing. She has already written two books, namely *A Guest in God's World: Memories of Madagascar* and *The Detour: An Off-Road Safari.* Two other books are in preparation, she says. The third book will be published in 2013. A fourth is in the planning stage and will actually be written during her mission in Mauritius. This book – which she has already found the title – The Widow's Mite and the Bishop's Miter – will relate to her priestly life and that of her husband. In this book, "I intend to show how two different colors can marry in weaving the tapestry of the Church of God," she says, and of course, she hopes to make a nod to the mission home.

Appendix B

Induction Service of
The Rev. Dr. Patricia McGregor
St. Simon's the Fisherman, Tamarin, Mauritius

September 23, 2012
Delivered by Archbishop of the Province of the
Indian Ocean and Bishop of the Anglican Diocese of
Mauritius, Ian Ernest

This is my whole life, O Lord
To know your word and to teach it
To know your word and live it
Teach me, O Lord
To proclaim what you teach
To live how you live
Through Jesus Christ. Amen.

In the name of the Father, and of the Son and of the Holy Spirit. Amen.

The prayer I have just said are from Bishop Kwashi from Nigeria and it expresses the essence of the priestly ministry that Rev. Patsy McGregor is called to serve and hold. Before going further, I wish to express publicly my gratitude to:

1. The Rt. Rev. Samoela Jaona Ranarivelo – Bishop of Antananarivo, Madagascar

2. The Rt. Rev. Leo Frade – Bishop of the Diocese of Southeast Florida

3. Mrs. Denise Cox – Society of Anglican Missionaries and Senders

4. Mr. Syd Verinder – President of People Reaching People

For accepting to release her so that she is able to serve The Anglican Diocese of Mauritius. This indeed underlines the ability for us Anglicans to build up bonds of friendship in spite of the vast distances that separates us from each other.

The sharing of experience between Diocese and Provinces of the Anglican Communion enriches us and express the catholicity of our Church – the Church to whom God has entrusted his mission.

The appointment of Rev. Patsy McGregor as the Rector of the new parish of St. Simon the Fisherman in Tamarin makes history, following the Provincial and the Diocesan resolution made in 2006 & 2008 respectively concerning the acceptance of ordaining women to the diaconate and to the priesthood. We are today welcoming for the first time a woman as a member of the clergy of the Diocese of Mauritius. It has its roots founded in the work of the Holy Spirit which tunes in to the vision that God has for the Anglican Diocese of Mauritius. In the Epistle to the Roman, we are told that the Christian mindset is to be reshaped by the Power of the Gospel and the concern of the age to come rather than the passing fashion of this age. Only by such sanctifying renewal the Christian is made sufficiently sensitive to deserve the behavior that is God's Will in each situation.

"Do not conform to the pattern of this world, but be transformed by the renewing of your mind. Then you will be able to test and approve what God's will is-his good, pleasing and perfect will..." (Rom 12v2) NIV

Rev. Patsy McGregor is leaving her husband Bishop Todd McGregor living in Tulear, Madagascar – it is God who sent her here. Being far away from her homeland, from her family, from her friends, from her culture may be for her a thorn in the flesh. It's not easy to be a servant of God in a foreign land. But here again, Paul in his letter to the Corinthians clearly describes the depth of God's sustenance toward those he called to serve him.

I quote: "Here was given me a thorn in my flesh, three times I pleaded with the Lord to take it away from me. But he said to me: 'My grace is sufficient for you for my power is made perfect in weakness."

I wish Rev. Patsy on behalf of the Diocese to welcome you here as a sister – we invite you to be part of our family here in Mauritius. The grace that God bestows on you today is indeed our love for you and our gratitude to you for accepting to be a servant of Christ in our midst.

The Scripture reminds that we are imbued with gifts to be witnesses of Christ to the world. It also states that all of us belonging to the body of Christ – are responsible for sharing the gospel where we live and among the people with whom we associate every day.

Rom 12:6 NIV: "We have different gifts, according to the grace given to each of us. If your gift is prophesying, then prophesy in accordance with your faith;"

In a conversation that I have had with Rev. Patsy and in the interview given to "Le Mauricien" yesterday, Rev. Patsy shared that the vision that God has entrusted to her is to be an enabler, a teacher, a reconciler and a listener. This is how as followers of Christ we should act with people whom we serve.

But are we doing it...and are we doing it successfully? These questions are relevant, both for you and me – Do we have the right motivations, attitudes, strategies and message to evangelize the world around us effectively? In other words, are we truly ready for Christian Service?

This induction service is meant to act as a starter to the ministry of Rev. Patsy McGregor here in Black River. This should create for her the springboard from which she would have an overview of the task that lies ahead. Her presence here since the 17th of August has enabled her to possess a grasp of Mauritian life – its realities, its challenges, it's richness and its weaknesses. I am sure that with our prayers, her new calling here will:

1) Give here the opportunity to enable you as the people of God to grow into the maturity of Christ.

2) Encourage you to be reconciled to God and to one another in spite of the complexities and the paradox of human nature.

3) Sustain this Church to be an agent for healing and transformation.

What then should be the motivation of Rev. Patsy McGregor and of the people of God here if the vision for this Church as described above is to be realized?

I am convinced that it has to be founded on the motivation of Christ for ministry in Galilee.

The ministry of Jesus in Galilee was motivated by a powerful love and drive to seek out people who need help, hope and deliverance from sin and disease. When he saw the crowd, he had compassion on them because they were harassed and helpless, like sheep without a shepherd. Jesus took the initiative and driven by selfless love for people, went with vigor and enthusiasm to seek and save the lost. People were coming to him not because of his rhetorical skills and miracles but rather because of his attitude toward the people and of his attention to their needs.

As your Bishop, this is my struggle and my vision. It is my dream that we are all called to be transforming agents – the mandate of God at our Synod is to Equip, Empower, Evangelize – is not *my* plan but the plan for the People of God living in this diocese. It clearly draws its inspiration from the motivation of Christ – parishes are called to build up on this plan and to organize the life of the Parish as per the needs of its specific reality. I encourage you my brothers and sisters to live up to Christ's expectation. The ministry is not only a task that belongs to Bishops and priests – it belongs to the People of

God – to you who have been baptized and who at confirmation have agreed to be Servants to the Mission Dei – Mission of God.

We Anglicans, who had by the grace of God established this new parish of St. Simon should continue it and consolidate its calling with passion and a sense of abnegation. Today it is our responsibility to take the Gospel to this part of Mauritius and to act as detergents so that we be cleaned from harassment, helplessness, despair and hopelessness. This world needs caring leadership. This should be our objective.

What would be Christ's attitude toward the people of today? Has his attitude changed with the passage of time? No. The compassion of Jesus and his understanding transcends time, generations and culture and the distance between ancient Galilee and modern Mauritius.

It is a fact that certain notion of life have evolved but the basic needs of Society remain – and so does the compassion of Christ. Together with you, as your Bishop, let us challenge ourselves – let Christ be our teacher, let us strive to possess, if we want to be enablers, reconcilers, and healers a view of the world with the same sensibility and care as Jesus had.

And here I wish to ask for forgiveness if the clergy and I have shown toward you a lack of compassion in the manner we serve you. I wish here to also say to the clergy who are my collaborators that my prayer is to be able to be with them as a brother, as a pastor and as a compassionate servant. This is indeed my prayer.

The compassion of Christ which made him an enabler, a reconciler and a healer was not static. It was translated into dynamic intervention and loving action. Jesu met the needs of the people with 3 simple but powerful strategies.

> Nurturing
> Exhorting
> Sharing

Jesus knew just what the people in his day needed – solid – God – based teaching. He taught them truth that set them free. Today itself we are invaded with notions that can pervade the truth.

Books and films are produced to sling mud on the life our Lord Jesus Christ and his teachings. It seems that it could threaten the teachings of the church – not at all, actually it comes as an opportunity for us to teach, to talk about the truth that sets us free. Banning the book and the film will increase the appetite of those who are soul-searching. Let our Churches as synagogues become places where we could invite people who have read books or seen films to come and to be in dialogue with those whose faith is founded on Jesus who is the Way, the Truth and the Life. The primary message of the Gospel is to be brought to light – the ministry of Jesus triggered a dynamic spiritual renaissance in Galilee – something he surely longs to do again through us, through the Ministry of Rev. Patsy McGregor and of your parish here in Black River.

We all here have to learn from Jesus. Here in this Diocese, we take time before we decide to commit ourselves for a good cause. Let us follow the example of Jesus. It would be for us a real test of readiness for meeting people's needs. We shall fall short in our efforts to bring people to Christ, to involve them in the church, and to hold them for the kingdom – if we lack authentic Christian compassion.

So the test is:

1) Are we motivated by Christ's selfless love?

2) Are we witnessing with the compassionate attitude of Jesus?

3) Are we employing his 3 dynamic strategies
   Nurturing – exhorting – sharing

I believe today that with this induction, and with the specific calling of Rev. Patsy, Christ is challenging all of us. He is inviting us to get involved, to pray for and to recruit others to work alongside him in loving service. The potential exists but there's still a shortage of workers. So, my invitation to all of you this evening is let's all go to work for Jesus who has done the ultimate work for us, on the Cross of Calvary.

Today, let the Anglican Church in Black River be a leading organization that can transform this region and set in the kingship of Christ. Amen.

Appendix C

On the front lines of ministry in Madagascar, spiritual warfare was unrelenting. I found these two prayers helpful to keep me spiritually fit and able to do the work and ministry we were called to do.

A Prayer for Protection

To be prayed before Ministry
The Rev. Dr. Francis MacNutt
www.christianhealingmin.org

In the name of Jesus Christ and by the power of his Cross and his Blood, we bind up the power of any evil spirits and command them not to block our prayers. We bind up the powers of earth, air, water, fire, the netherworld and the satanic forces of nature.

We break an curses, hexes or spells sent against us and declare them null and void. We break the assignments of any spirits sent against us and send them to Jesus to deal with them as he will. Lord, we ask you to bless our enemies by sending your Holy Spirit to lead them to repentance and conversion.

Furthermore, we bind all interaction and communication in the world of evil spirits as it affects us and our ministry.

We ask for the protection of the shed blood of Jesus Christ over _____.

Thank you, Lord, for your protection and send your angels, especially St. Michael, the Archangel, to help us in the battle. We ask you to guide us in our prayers; share with us your Spirit's power and compassion. Amen

Prayer to be Set Free

To be prayed following ministry
The Rev. Dr. Francis MacNutt
www.christianhealingmin.org

Lord Jesus, thank you for sharing with us your wonderful ministry of healing and deliverance. Thank you for the healings we have seen and experienced today.

We realize that the sickness and evil we encounter is more than our humanity can bear, so cleanse of any sadness, negativity or despair that we may have picked up. If our ministry has tempted us to anger, impatience or lust, cleanse us of those temptations and replace them with love, joy and peace.

If any evil spirits have attached themselves to us or oppressed us in any way, we command you, spirits of earth, air, fire, water, the netherworld or the satanic forces of nature, to despair –now—and go straight to Jesus Christ for him to deal with you as he will.

Come Holy Spirit renew us—fill us anew with your power, your life and your joy. Strengthen us where we have felt weak, and clothe us with your light. Fill us with life. Lord Jesus, please send your holy angels to minister to us and our families – guard us and protect us from all sickness, harm and accidents. (Give us a safe trip home.)

We praise you now and forever, Father, Son and Holy Spirit, and we ask these things in Jesus' Holy Name that he may be glorified. Amen

Bibliography

Benner, David G. *Surrender to Love.* Downers Grove, Il.: International Varsity Press, 2003.

Bradt, Hilary. Madagascar: The Bradt Travel Guide, Ninth Edition. Guilford, CT: The Globe Pequot Press, Inc., 2008.

Brown, Brené. *Dare to Lead.* New York: Random House, 2018.

Butterfield, Jane (editor), *The Scripture of their Lives: Stories of Mission Companions Today.* Church Publishing, 2006.

Eye Witness Travel Guides: Paris. A DK Publishing Book, 1997 revised.

Foster, Richard J. *Prayer: Finding the Heart's True Home.* San Francisco : Harper, 2002.

Friesen, James G., E. James Wilder, Anne M. Bierling, Rick Koepke, and Maribeth

Poole. *Living from the Heart Jesus Gave You.* Pasadena, CA: Shepherd's House Inc. 2000, revised.

Grogan, Brian. *Finding God in All Things.* Dublin, Ireland: Messenger Publications, 1996.

Hall, Christopher A., Carolyn Arends, and Renovaré. *The Reservoir: A Fifteen Month Week-day Devotional for Individuals and Groups,* Renovare Publishers.

Holy Bible, New International Version (NIV), Biblica, 1978.

Joyce, Timothy. *Celtic Christianity: A Sacred Tradition, A Vision of Hope.* Maryknoll, New York: Orbis Books, 1998.

Kendrick, Stephen and Alex Kendrick. *The Love Dare.* B & H Publishing Group, 2008.

Lake, Frank and Emil Brunner, Understanding the Cycle of Grace," cited in *The Reservoir.*

MacBeth, Sybil. *Praying in Color: Drawing a New Path to God.* Brewster, MA:Paraclete Press, 2007.

Mbiti, John S. *Introduction to African Religion.* Heinemann, 1991.

Moore, Karen. *Blessing from God for Women.* Christian Art Gifts, Inc. 2012.

Norris, Michelle. "Why the Future Should be Female: Examining Women's Work Over Centuries," *National Geographic*, November, 2019.

The New Oxford Annotated Bible with Apocrypha, New Revised Standard Version (NRSV), Augmented Third Edition, Oxford Press, 2018.

Nouwen, Henri J.M., *Can You Drink the Cup?* Ave Maria Press, 1996.

_____.*The Way of the Heart.* Editorial Lumen, 2008.

Parker, Russ. *Rediscovering the Ministry of Blessing.* Spck Publishing, 2014.

Peterson, Eugene H. *The Message: Bible in Contemporary Language.* Navpress, 2007.

Proust, Marcel. *The Prisoner: In Search of Lost Time,* Volume 5, Penguin Classics Deluxe Edition.

Rath, Tom. *Strengthsfinder 2.0*. Gallup Press, 2007.

Thiele, Rob and George David Weiss. Composers: *What a Wonderful World*, 1967.

Thurman, Howard. *The Living Wisdom of Howard Thurman: A Visionary for Our Time*. Audio CD, Sounds True, 2010.

Vanauken, Sheldon. *A Severe Mercy*, 1977.

Wilder, E. James, Edward M. Khouri, Chris M. Coursey and Shelia D. Sutton. *Joy Starts Here: The Transformation Zone*. Pasadena, CA: Shepherd's House Inc., 2014.

Young, Sarah. *Jesus Lives, Seeing His Love in Your Heart*. Thomas Nelson, 2009.

Endnotes

1   Luke 21:2

2   Sybil MacBeth, Praying in Color. This is a powerful and gentle tool to practice communication with God. In 2008 in Ankilifaly, as a way of engaging the community, I introduced Praying in Color to the youth. About twenty of us met a few times a week in the half-built church right on the main street of the village. This form of evangelism turned into discipleship. Since that time, one of the young participants has become the first woman priest in the Diocese of Toliara and others have developed into local leaders. When you go to Madagascar, you can visit the resource center and see the more than 1000 prayer cards that have nourished our spiritual growth. Praying in Color can help with prayers of discernment, Lectio Divina and memorizing Scripture.

3   Marcel Proust, In Search of Lost Time: La Prisonniere

4   Martin Luther King, Jr.

5   Miaraka: A Time to Dance. This original musical production co-authored by The Rev. Patsy McGregor and Collette Maurel, is a modern-day story of Mary Magdalene. It was born through darkness, heartache, a light of hope and the need to awaken global consciousness of the ongoing cycle of poverty, human trafficking and prostitution. This production has come together (Miaraka, the Malagasy word for 'together') through the hard work of our production team and friends. It has been performed in Mauritius, Madagascar, South Africa (at the invitation of Desmond Tutu) and the USA.

6   Isaiah 61:1

7   Joshua 1:9

8   Romans 1:16

[9] Brené Brown, Dare to Lead, 10.

[10] Brown, 19.

[11] Brown, 86.

[12] Tom Rath, Strengthsfinder 2.0 "Activator," 41.

[13] Sheldon Vanauken, Severe Mercy, 196. Quoting correspondence with C.S. Lewis

[14] Hebrews 6:18-19

[15] Jeremiah 29:1

[16] Psalm 5:12

[17] What a Wonderful World. Jazz song popularized by Louis Armstrong and written by Bob Thiele (as "George Douglas"} and George David Weiss.

[18] Romans 8:28

[19] Psalm 31:24

[20] Isaiah 40:11

[21] Matthew 22:37-40

[22] https://en.wikipedia.org/wiki/Madagascar; https://www.cia.gov/the-world-factbook/countries/Madagascar; and personal experience

[23] Stephen Kendrick & Alex Kendrick, The Love Dare, 137

[24] Matthew 25:35-36.

[25] Brown, 4.

[26] Judges 6:11-21

[27] In Christianity orthopraxy means "correct practice" or "correct behavior" as opposed to orthodoxy which refers to "correct teaching" or correct doctrine"

[28] Ephesians 4:1

[29] Judges 6:22-23

[30] Hebrews 11:32

[31] Richard Foster, Prayer: Finding the Heart's True Home, 243.

32 Foster, 245.

33 Celtic Christianity: Christianity first reached the Celtic people of Ireland and Britain as early as the second century C.E. and began to blossom by the fifth century. This encounter between the Christian religion and Celtic tradition engendered a deep and distinctive spirituality rooted in the goodness of creation and taught that the Godhead contains both feminine and masculine attributes. This contrast to dualistic strains of Christian thought, which prioritize spirit over matter and emphasizes the masculine aspects of God, Celtic Christianity emphasizes the sacred essence of all creation and Creation, like Scripture, reveals God's heart. Likewise, The Celtic way of Christianity emphasizes the essential goodness of humanity, with less focus on the Augustinian view of original sin. The Celtic Christian perspective sees the presence of God infused in the community and in daily life, so that in everyday happenings and ordinary ways, any object, any job of work, can become a place for an encounter with God. This community-based and creation -based tradition of Christianity has been especially embraced in our ministry in Madagascar.

34 Ezekiel 22:30

35 Edward Everett Hale

36 Saint Teresa of Calcutta

37 Saint Teresa of Calcutta

38 Saint Teresa of Calcutta

39 Henri J. M. Nouwen, Can You Drink the Cup? 28.

40 1 John 4:18

41 Frank Lake and Emil Brunner, "Understanding the Cycle of Grace," cited in The Reservoir, 17. See endnote 67.

42 Russ Parker, Rediscovering the Ministry of Blessing, 39. Referring to Matthew 5:3-12

43 Parker, 42.

44 Praying in Color. See reference in endnote 2

45   Psalm 89:15

46   Foster, 247.

47   E. James Wilder, Edward M. Khouri, Chris M. Coursey, and Shelia D. Sutton, Joy Starts Here: The Transformation Zone

48   E. James Wilder et al.

49   2 Chronicles 7:14

50   2 Corinthians 12:9

51   E. James Wilder et al.

52   Henri J. M. Nouwen, The Way of the Heart

53   Acts 3:6

54   Parker, 42

55   James 2:5

56   Leo Buscaglia

57   Conversation with Bev Erasmus

58   Isaiah 41:10

59   St. Augustine of Hippo

60   Kendrick and Kendrick, 166

61   3 John 4

62   2 Thessalonians 1:3-4

63   Ashish Ram, January 5, 2007

64   Genesis 9:20-23

65   1 Corinthians 1:10, The Message

66   The Reservoir: A Fifteen Month Devotional Week-day Devotional for Individuals and Groups, Christopher A. Hall, Carolyn Arends and Renovaré

67   Genesis 1

68   Matthew 3:17; Mark 1:11

69   Karen Moore, Blessings from God for Women, 12

70   John 14:27

[71] Pope Francis, Rome: Angelus Address, August 30, 2020.

[72] Sarah Young, Jesus Lives, 310

[73] Francis MacNutt. Prayer for Protection: to be prayed before ministry and Prayer to be Set Free: To be prayed following ministry. See Appendices C and D

[74] Ephesians 1:20-21

[75] Isaiah 41:10

[76] George Bernard Shaw, winner of 1925 Nobel Prize for literature

[77] Psalm 91:4

[78] David C Benner, Surrender to Love, 12.

[79] Pope Francis, Rome: Angelus Address, July 26, 2020.

[80] Colossians 1:11, The Message

[81] Rath

[82] Ephesians 2:10

[83] Proverbs 3:5

[84] National Geographic (November 2019), Michelle Norris, "Why the Future Should be Female: Examining Women's Work Over Centuries," 31.

[85] Eleanor Roosevelt

[86] Pope Francis, excerpt from a webinar to a Women's Consultation Group of the Pontifical Council for Culture, October 7, 2020

[87] John 15:15

[88] Galatians 5:22-23, NRSV

[89] Conversation with the Rt. Rev. Dr. Todd McGregor

[90] Proverbs 3:5

[91] https://www.vocabulary.com/

[92] Jane Butterfield (editor), The Scripture of Their Lives: Stories of Mission Companions Today, (foreword) Desmond Tutu, ix.

93 Tutu, Scripture of Their Lives, xi

94 Howard Thurman, The Living Wisdom of Howard Thurman: A Visionary for Our Time

95 Hilary Bradt, Madagascar: The Bradt Travel Guide, Ninth Edition

96 Ephesians 6:10-18 The Armor of God: 10 Finally, be strong in the Lord and in his mighty power. 11 Put on the full armor of God, so that you can take your stand against the devil's schemes. 12 For our struggle is not against flesh and blood, but against the rulers, against the authorities, against the powers of this dark world and against the spiritual forces of evil in the heavenly realms. 13 Therefore put on the full armor of God, so that when the day of evil comes, you may be able to stand your ground, and after you have done everything, to stand. 14 Stand firm then, with the belt of truth buckled around your waist, with the breastplate of righteousness in place, 15 and with your feet fitted with the readiness that comes from the gospel of peace. 16 In addition to all this, take up the shield of faith, with which you can extinguish all the flaming arrows of the evil one. 17 Take the helmet of salvation and the sword of the Spirit, which is the word of God.18 And pray in the Spirit on all occasions with all kinds of prayers and requests. With this in mind, be alert and always keep on praying for all the Lord's people.

97 Warren Wiersbe

98 L'Express, September 22, 2012

99 Lamba – a Malagasy word for a large piece of cloth used as a cape by men and a dress by women

100 Paris: Eyewitness Travel Guides, "Opéra de Paris Bastille," 98.

101 John S. Mbiti, Introduction to African Religion

102 Winston Churchill

103 Friedrich Nietzsche

104 Benner,16.

105 Philippians 4:12

106   Parker, 38.

107   Winston Churchill

108   Philippians 1:29

109   2 Timothy 4:6-8

110   Meister Eckhardt

111   I Corinthians 13:3-4

112   Ruth 1:16

113   Frank A. Clark

114   Martin Luther King, Jr.

115   Conversations with Bev Erasmus and the Rt. Rev. Samitiana
       Razafindralambo

116   Oliver Wendell Holmes, Sr.

117   Frank A. Clark

118   Joshua 1:9

119   Romans 1:16

120   Brown

121   Philippians 4:12

122   Brown

123   Ephesians 4:12

124   Kendrick and Kendrick, 166.

125   Genesis 1

126   Isaiah 41:10

127   Timothy 2:2

128   The Rt. Rev. Dr. Todd McGregor

129   Proverbs 3:5

130   Ephesians 4:1